Guardianwork

Guardianwork

by

Ian Carpenter

Beautiful
Books

First published by Beautiful Books Limited.

www.beautiful-books.co.uk

Beautiful Books Limited
36–38 Glasshouse Street
London W1B 5DL

ISBN 9781905636662

9 8 7 6 5 4 3 2 1

Cover design by Ian Pickard.
Printed in Great Britain by CPI Mackays, Chatham ME5 8TD

For Nicola

Sunday 30th September 2007

I am 34 years old and I'm employed as a property manager for a Basildon-based property management company. It's all glitz and glamour. I had an idea last night. I was leafing through the Guardian Work section when it came to me:

I am going to apply for every single job in this newspaper.

Fully expecting to be met with doubt and concern, I sent a text message to Simon, who is also a property manager at the same company. I got this reply:

That is a brilliant idea. Put me as your reference.

And so it starts...

The front page of the Guardian Work section promises 100s of jobs including: Management, General, HR, Retail, Sales, Marketing & PR, Creative & Media, New Media (what's that all about?), Secretarial, IT & T (what's that second 't' for?), Courses, Education, Social Care, Public, and Tenders. Surely I can do all of these things. OK, the first job is for the NHS:

You can go to work, or come to life

Brilliant. I like life.

Here in the NHS, we bring commissioning to life every day

What?!

Because it's not just about the numbers or the services or increasing efficiency. It's about all of this and more: we see improved commissioning as integral to better funding and delivery of public services. So, the bottom line is, in an organisation that employs 1.3 million people, has an operating budget of £90 billion and is the largest of any kind in Europe, commissioning roles here are vital to life itself.

Gateway to leadership programme

It's not work, it's life.

Fantastic! The first job is not even work. It's life, apparently. I can do that. I can live. This is definitely the job for me. Commissioning. It really can't be that hard. My partner Nicky is an art teacher at a local comprehensive school. She was once commissioned by a friend of ours to draw a picture for her flat. All she had to do was say 'Nicky, can you do me a drawing for my front room?' Simple. I can do this. The website has a 'meet Gateway alumni' section, let's see what kind of person commissions for the NHS –

Joe Gibson: Director for the Strategy and Implementation for the NHS in East Lancashire.

Apparently Joe is ex-RAF. He's responsible for the direction of various projects. These projects will 'reconfigure health and social care across the region and will deliver a 21st century health care for East Lancashire'. This is all good. I like health care and I like the 21st century. Joe is also an aficionado of Shrewsbury Town Football Club, swimming and skiing. To relax, he enjoys walking in the hills of Shropshire, gardening and classical music. I like Joe. I think I could work with him, and possibly discuss viburnums and gladioli with him too. You have to apply online and they need a 'user ID name*'. Hmm, the first challenge. How about 'guardianwork'? Apparently there's a pre-screening to see if I am eligible to complete the application form... what?! OK, I'll log in and go to the pre-screening section –

Pre-Screening
Which area of the gateway to leadership programme are you interested in? *

○ **Commissioning**
○ **General**
◉ **Both**

Do you have a level of educational attainment that is at

or above Bachelors degree level (Second class Honours), OR equivalent? *

◉ **Yes**
○ **No**

Do you have 4 or more years (or equivalent) senior management experience? *

○ **Yes**
◉ **No**

Do you have experience in leading, managing and developing at a senior level? *

◉ **Yes**
○ **No**

Do you have experience at a senior level of working within a complex project management environment? *

○ **Yes**
◉ **No**

Do you have the unrestricted right to work in the UK? *

◉ **Yes**
○ **No**

Questions marked with an '*' are compulsory and must be completed before you submit your appliction.

That seems fair enough. I should at least be eligible to apply. Hello? What's this?:

Thank you for your application to the NHS Gateway to Leadership programme.

We appreciate the amount of time that you have contributed to this process however I regret to inform you that on this occasion it did not meet the required level. We will not therefore be taking your application any further.

Due to the large number of applications to the Scheme this year we are unfortunately unable to offer any individual feedback.

[...] Thank you again for your interest in the NHS, and may we take this opportunity to wish you the best of luck in your future career.

<u>Logout</u>

I have fallen at the first hurdle. Apparently I'm not eligible to apply. This is not going to be as easy as I thought it would be. I've been at my quest for only 3 hours and I've already received my first rejection. I don't mind being rejected but I do object to being rejected by an organisation that can't spell application. OK, moving swiftly on to job 2:

City and Guilds – A great place to work.
Recently awarded Best Investor in Excellence in London, City & Guilds brings real benefits to economies, businesses and individuals worldwide by setting the standard for vocational education and providing skills for a brighter future.

The role is Qualification Support Manger. I can support Qualifications. I've supported worse in my time.

Educated to degree level

Tick.

Excellent communication skills

Tick – I once talked until 5 in the morning.

Experience in project management

Tick(ish).

An understanding of current developments and trends in education

Tick. See above, my partner is a teacher. The trend in her school is for Rich Tea biscuits.

So, I have to send my CV to Marike Dippenaar. What a fabulous name. Well, Marike, you are about to be the recipient of my first application. I don't know whether to play it straight or be completely up front about what I'm doing. If my covering letter were along the lines of 'Dear Marike, I am applying to every single job that appeared in the Guardian on the 29th September 2007. Would you please peruse my CV and see if I am the man for you? Kind regards, Ian Carpenter', it might not go down too well. I'm not actually looking for a new job. I haven't even considered what would happen if I got an interview. Could I really go to City and Guilds with a straight face and convince them that I wanted to support their qualifications? Hmmm... We'll see what happens. I have to find my CV. I haven't updated it since I got the job with the property management company. I've been comfortable for over 14 months. I manage properties in London without having to do the commute into London every day. Let's bring things up to date –

Responsible for the management of 30 residential properties in central London. This involves day to day management of the properties. I deal with leaseholders and contractors on a daily basis, both face to face and on the telephone. I manage four members of staff. I chair Annual General Meetings with Residents' Associations.

There. That should do it, now the letter –

Dear Marike

I am writing following your recent advertisement in The Guardian for a Qualification Support Manager. I am passionate about education. I am a strong believer that it is never too late for anyone to learn. I personally went back to university at the age of 30 to complete a degree that I had started 12 years earlier. I have ten years experience in the banking sector, and 18 months experience in property management. I look forward to hearing from you soon.

Yours sincerely

Ian Carpenter

I've just checked my outbox. Instead of attaching my CV, I attached the opening pages of this project. Oops. Oh well, let's see what happens. I'm feeling slightly disappointed about being rejected by the NHS earlier. I was really looking forward to working with Joe Gibson.

Monday 1st October 2007

I woke up this morning at 3.00am. I think this thing could become slightly obsessive. I finally got off to sleep and it was 7.20 before I knew it. I've had a cough for about two weeks and, as a result, I've pulled a muscle in my side. Officially man-flu. I couldn't get out of bed at first, as I couldn't sit up. I had to roll out sideways before climbing up the wall. I was excited though. I couldn't wait to get to work. I'd printed the first pages of this thing and wanted to see what the reaction would be.

I presented last night's efforts to Simon and his response was good. He seems to think I'm on to something. I spent most of the day wondering whether I should really see it through, but I showed some of my other colleagues the project and they all seemed to like it. So I've decided to go ahead with it for the time being at least. And I think I'll set up some kind of blog...

Tuesday 2nd October 2007

I suddenly realise how difficult this project is going
to be. I spent a total of two and a half hours travelling
to and from work today. This meant I got in around
6.45pm and by the time I'd had dinner – minced beef
pie and roast potatoes – it was 9.35. I'm three days into
my quest and I've still only done two jobs, one of which
I was disqualified from even applying for. Last night,
I spent the evening setting up http://guardianwork.
blogspot.com. It's not very good, but it's a start. I've
uploaded the first instalment of Guardianwork and it
seems that everything is accessible and pretty easy to
understand. I've also sent an email to The Guardian
newspaper to see if they're interested in my project.
None of this detracts from the fact that I need to get
on with applying for these jobs:

Holy Cross Centre Trust: Sustainable Change through innovation

Immediately alarm bells start to ring. This is a charity.
Should I be wasting their time in applying for their jobs,
which I don't even want? Is that ethical? Well, a challenge
is a challenge. All is fair in love, war and 'The trust that
grew out of the King's Cross Community's direct action
to the problems and needs that they saw around them'.
Besides, I'm sure their HR person has had to send many

a rejection letter. They have, however, presented me with a problem: there are five jobs advertised:

1 Co-production/timebank worker

1 Senior Support, time recovery (STR) worker

1 Part time intermediate STR worker

1 Part time mental health Promotion and Community Link worker

They're also looking to employ 'sessionally paid A1 and V1 qualified' people. I have to admit I'm a bit thrown by these positions. For a start, I have absolutely no idea what they mean (apart from maybe the Community Link worker). Secondly, should I apply for each job individually or send my CV in with a covering note for all five jobs? All five would certainly add to my tally and I really do need to get a move on. I have to email recruitment@hcct.org.uk for an application form, so here goes –

Dear Madam/Sir

I notice that you have five jobs advertised in the Guardian Work section dated 29/9/07. I would be grateful if you could send me details of how to apply for these positions?

Kind regards

Ian Carpenter

Great!!! 7 jobs applied for, with only one rejection. That is a non-success rate of 14.3%, a rate of which I am particularly proud, especially only three days in. OK, I feel a little guilty about the charity thing. I've vowed to send a donation to the Holy Cross Centre Trust. I'll reimburse them for stamps etc. I am absolutely determined to get to the end of page one this evening. Only six more jobs to go. Given that I applied for five in a single email, this should be nothing. Next:

The Zygos Partnership is looking for a research consultant.

I can research; I have been known to study for various periods of time.

You will have achieved high honours at a leading university

Ok –

Dear Karen

I am writing to apply for the Research Consultant Position advertised in the Guardian on the 29/9/07.

As you can see from my attached CV, I have a strong academic background and very many years (perhaps too many!) working in the private sector.

I hope you will consider me for your positions.

Kind regards

Ian Carpenter

I have to admit though, the organisation does sound a bit like a Masonic cult, so we shall have to tread carefully. I haven't reached the bottom of the page yet and it's now 10.30pm. Jeremy Paxman is calling. By the way, the answer to the maths questions on University Challenge are always 1, 0 or −1.

Wednesday 3rd October 2007

I HAVE MY FIRST RESPONSE FROM A HUMAN BEING! (sorry about the capital letters, but this is a momentous achievement):

Dear Ian,

Thank you for your recent email application for the position of Research Consultant at The Zygos Partnership. We will contact you no later than the end of October in reference to this role.

In the meantime, thank you for your interest.

Kind regards,

Karren

Karren Price
Assistant to Dr John Viney
The Zygos Partnership

I take back all previous comments about the Zygos Partnership. Thank you Karren. And so friendly! The way that my flippant 'kind regards' sign off has been mirrored is pure brilliance. So, I will hear back from them by the end of the month. Today has been fairly interactive on all fronts really. I sent an email to my friend Stew to see if he's interested in what I'm doing. I received the following response:

Every time I talk to you you tell me how busy
you are!!!!

Stew

Yes, but do you like the idea?

It's your own fault for reading a pretentious,
leftie, quasi intellectual rag like The Guardian!

Stew

ps They can't spell either

He has a point. More observant readers will have noticed
a typo in the opening paragraph. 'The Guardian Wrok
section' was deliberate *[Corrected by present editor. Sorry
Ian, it's on the very first page and what about those who didn't
read far enough in to realise it was a deliberate mistake? Ed.]*.
Anyway, the excitement of receiving a human response
shouldn't divert me from applying for more jobs: The
Scottish Adoption – Chief Executive. Woah. This is big
stuff. I really don't have a social work background, or
any financial management experience at a high level...
No, wait! – I worked in a bank! And I did a social policy
degree – come on! This is definitely the job for me. Plus
they're offering a Final Salary Pension Scheme (their
capitals). Here goes –

Dear Sandra

I am writing regarding your vacancy for a Chief Executive. I would be grateful if you could send me more details regarding this position, and possibly an information pack.

Kind regards

Ian Carpenter

UK Sport want a 'COACHING CONSULTANT qualified to degree level with a good knowledge of elite level sports in the UK'. No problem, I watched rugby only last week in the pub –

Dear Madam/Sir

I would like to apply for the position of Coaching Consultant as advertised in the Guardian dated 29/09/07. I have no experience in this area, however I am qualified to degree level and I do like watching elite sport.

I have attached my Curriculum Vitae for your perusal.

Kind regards

Ian Carpenter

The International Institute of Communications is looking

for a Director General. This is a part time position. Well, really, how long can it take to direct communications? –

'You speak!'

'Now you speak!'

It can't be that hard. I reckon I could do this job, research for the Zygos Partnership, *and* be a part time STR worker for the Holy Cross Centre Trust. Let's have a look at the site –

BACKGROUND
The IIC was formed in 1969 at Ditchley Park in the UK. The underlying objective was to provide a non-partisan organisation to enable international debate of all kinds on the increasingly complex world of communications. The IIC's mission is to provide a global framework for dialogue and to promote access to communications for all peoples of the world. It is an international, interdisciplinary, independent, not-for-profit membership organisation and a registered charity. Its funding comes from subscriptions, donations and projects. It is governed by an international Board of Directors and advised by a select number of Trustees.

Great. Another charity. And, yes, I will donate stamps etc. if I get a response.

APPLICATIONS
Please contact Sebastian Mann with an expression of your interest and most relevant experience along with a full CV and details of two referees.

No problem, Sebastian –

Dear Sebastian

I would like to express my interest in your vacancy for Director General of the Institute of Communications. Please find attached my CV for your perusal. As you can see I am able to communicate in a direct way.

Kind regards

Ian Carpenter

Thursday 4th October 2007

We have a spider that lives in our dining room. It lives there quite happily. Throughout the day, it hides behind the picture rail by the window in the dining room. No one would know it was there. I'm a smoker and the only place I smoke at home is in the dining room. The spider only comes out when I get in from work and sit down for a smoke by the back window. We have the world's first smoking spider. I hope one of the jobs will be working in the field of spider identification. Anyway, I have another response from a human! Sandra at Scottish Adoption emailed:

```
I am attaching pack - if you wish a hard copy
please e mail with your address, although there
is a postal strike today and it may not arrive
for some days.

Sandra
```

No kind regards. I don't think these people liked me. I'm having serious moral quandaries here. These people are doing some serious work in a serious area of Social Policy. It's actually a job I'd really like. I support everything they're doing. It makes my 'silly little boy' project look ridiculous. Should I leave it at that? Is a response enough? I'll leave it for now and move on –

Dear Ian,

Thank you for your email and interest in the DG position. We will be in touch soon after the closing date.

Best regards,

Sebastian Mann
Projects Executive
International Institute of Communications

Sebastian sends his best regards. I think he knows that I might not be taking this too seriously.

Monday 8th October 2007

The other day, while driving in Winchmore Hill, I was listening to Hawksbee and Jacobs on Talk Sport. They suggested a motorway game: France v England embodied by Norbert Dentressangle v Eddie Stobart lorries – how many of each can you spot? It's a great game, and I highly recommend it. I was kept amused from junction 26 to junction 29 on the M25 (The score was France 2 – England 0).

I did not apply for any jobs over the weekend. I've been hung up about this 'wasting the time of well meaning charities' thing. I was glad to get in to work and discuss it with some people. The consensus there is that I should continue to apply for every job, but I'm still not sure. I will definitely apply for all the jobs on the first page of the paper, after that who knows? Should I apply for only private sector jobs? Anyway, despite my misgivings, I need to get on with it – Handicap International are looking for a Director. Is 'handicap' PC? And they're looking to move to London in 2008 – fantastic, I can work in London. I will have:

Proven experience in the UK international development fundraising environment

Tick. I did raise money for children in need by dressing up as a cowboy.

Proven management skills

I can manage, thank you.

An ability to work collaboratively in an international environment

You should have seen me in 1990 in the international drama festival.

A commitment to working with disabled people

OK, I commit.

Excellent command of English and French

I actually do have an excellent command of French and English. This is the job I really want. No, really. This is why I did the Degree in EU Social Policy. I can speak French and I know about social policy stuff. I need to send a CV and a short covering letter to Ann Van Dyck –

Dear Ann

I am writing following your advertisement for Director. I am extremely passionate about the issues that your institution is dealing with. I studied for a Masters in EU Social policy. We were examining the way that the EU impacts on every member state's social policy issues. I look forward to hearing from you soon.

Yours sincerely

Ian Carpenter

Is that short enough? Now, the final job on page one. A two-in-one deal – do they think they're challenging me? Only two jobs? I once applied for five in one email, this is nothing –

Dear Amanda

You had a couple of jobs advertised in the Guardian recently. Am I the right person?

Kind regards

Ian Carpenter

Research Manager / Business Support Manager section done, and the end of the first page!!!

Tuesday 9th October 2007

OK, I've finished the first page. Where am I and what have I learned?

1. There is an organisation called the Zygos Partnership.

2. I probably shouldn't be wasting the time of well meaning charities.

3. The Norbert Dentressangle v Eddie Stobart game.

4. I have discovered a new kind of spider.

5. The NHS use a computer to reject possible applicants and they can't spell application.

I think that sums up everything so far, so I'll move on to page 2:

ten – join the revolution.

ten (lower case 't') are asking me to join a revolution! Are they are allowed to do this in a national newspaper? I'll bring my mate Che along for the interview, and Karl Marx can be my reference. OK ten, what are we going to revolutionise? Are you concerned with the race to the bottom? Are you against the war? What is it that we are set to revolutionise? Whatever it is, I'm in.

We are an award winning company with a passion to make a real difference to averting climate change and we are building a first rate team.

Right. Three jobs:

1. Marketing Operations Manager: *You will love the challenge of managing a sophisticated marketing plan.*

2. Operations Director: *You should have a demonstrable track record in managing a high quality service delivered across a wide range of functions.*

3. Analytics Manager: *You should be a real data junky.*

'A real data junky'? Am I in America? Anyhoo, I need to apply via their website –

Dear ten

I would love to be part of your revolution! Please find attached my Curriculum Vitae.

Kind regards

Ian Carpenter

Next one: Middlesex University have brought this challenge to one of its inevitable conclusions. They'd love me to be their Marketing and Recruitment Manager or Marketing Administrator. However, their closing date is the 8th of October. Which was yesterday. Blimey, you have to work quickly in this job application market. I suppose my three days off crisis of conscience thing didn't help. Should I apply anyway? Well, why not? –

Dear Middlesex University

I have missed the deadline for your two jobs in the Guardian dated 29th September 2007, sorry. Are you still looking for people?

Kind regards

Ian Carpenter

That's five jobs that done today. Good work, I reckon.

Wednesday 10th October 2007

I was in London today and nearly got run over by a police car. I was strolling along the Bayswater Road, the sun was shining, and I was heading for Lancaster Gate tube station. I could hear a police car siren in the environs, so had a good look around to make sure there wasn't one coming my way before I crossed the road. And then it came round the corner. I was smack, bang in the middle of the road. I thought my time was up. You know on Scooby Doo, when shaggy does that legs-moving-but-not-moving-forward thing? I did it!!! I was actually running on the spot, waiting to be hit by a speeding police car. I somehow made it to the other side of the road, but I did cause some amusement to the diners in the restaurant on the corner.

Today I received 2 emails:

We thank you for your interest in tenUK and will be in touch shortly.

Kind regards,

HR at tenUK

Thanks ten.

Please visit our website where all our current vacancies are listed and updated regularly

OK –

Recruitment

Thanks Middlesex University. Does anyone have a name? By the way, my smoking spider still hasn't appeared. Maybe she's died of spider lung cancer. And there's bad news for local livestock: Essex has been infested with bluetongue disease. Seriously, if ever a disease does what it says on the tin, that is it. What a fantastic name for a disease! –

Farmer: What has he got vet?

Vet: He has a blue tongue.

Farmer: Is it serious?

Vet: Yes, he has bluetongue disease.

Farmer: Oh.

If only every other disease was as brilliantly named. I mean BSE, or bovine spongiform encephalopathy. What a useless name that is. Who knows what symptoms you're going to get with that? I know 'bovine' relates to a cow, but 'spongiform'... what form does a spongi take? And it's hard enough just pronouncing 'encephalopathy', let alone fathoming what it means. And 'chicken pox'? How about 'itchy red spots that you have to scratch until you hurt disease'? Much better. So, all in all, I congratulate the person who named blue tongue disease. Good job. Anyway, on that note, the Health Professions Council are looking for a Lead Case Manager (x3) and Hearings Manager (x1). Was there really any need to put (x1)? What exactly does a lead case manager do? Do you have to manage cases made of lead? –

Dear Madam/Sir

I was intrigued by your job vacancy in the Guardian dated 29/9/07. Could you please tell me what is involved in managing cases that are made of lead? Is there some kind of protective suit that needs to be worn? I look forward to hearing from you soon.

Kind regards

Ian Carpenter

OK, the Merlin Housing association want a communications officer. No email address... I'll put that to one side for the moment. Next: this one's from St Paul's Cathedral! Oh, the closing date's 5th October. And anyway, I oughtn't be pestering religious organisations.

Thursday 11th October 2007

My smoking spider has reappeared! I think she must have just had a bit of a cough and so was laying off the fags for a while. Perhaps she took some spider Benylin (there are other spider cough medicines available – the honey and lemon spider Lemsip capsules come highly recommended). On the jobs front, Afghanaid want a UK Director – well I can't really apply for that one. Brad Insight are looking for a Research Supervisor and Research Executives:

A confident and approachable manner is critical in this role and familiarity with database systems would be an advantage.

I am fairly confident, and, I hope, approachable. And I'm familiar with databases and know I don't understand how they work –

Dear Susan

I read with some considerable interest the advertisement that you placed in The Guardian on the 29/09/07. As you can see from my attached CV, I can research. I can also supervise research. When I was at university, I used to watch the keen students in the library quite a lot. I hope that you will consider me for either position.

Kind regards

Ian Carpenter

Oops forgot to attach the CV –

It would have helped if I had attached my CV!!!

Kind regards

Ian carpenter

I'm never going to get the job now. Next: the British Ecological Society are looking for a Policy Officer:

The position offers an exciting opportunity for you to use your knowledge and experience of policy to develop the BES's role as an advocate for ecological science.

Gulp... the deadline for applications was noon today. Well I'm only a few hours late –

Dear Madam/Sir

I am late for applying for your position advertised in the Guardian dated 29/09/07. I really do apologise, but I have had a lot on my plate recently. Are you still looking for a Policy Officer, or have you appointed one this afternoon? I have attached my CV for your perusal, but I do appreciate that I am late in applying and that you may use it to mop up office spillages.

Kind regards

Ian Carpenter

SKI jobs want 'mountain people':

Ski Jobs: Knowledge is Powder.

Fantastic! 'Knowledge is powder'!!! Unfortunately there are literally thousands of jobs on their site... OK, I'm not going to apply for any of them as I am not good with heights and therefore mountains are probably not a good idea. Besides, if I got started on that, I'd never finish the quest. Thank you SKI JOBS, but no thanks. Good pun though. Next: Alliance supporting community action on AIDS in developing countries. No, I don't think so. This one looks the ticket though, and it's the last one on page 2:

ACM Advanced Currency Market SA.

What is an advanced currency? I thought the new twenty pound note was pretty advanced with its purple hue, but I think they're talking about something else here.

Fluent in English

This is in bold, so I must be on to a winner.

Experience in selling financial products

Erm, I did work in a bank for ten years. They want a photo, a CV and a covering letter. OK –

Dear Patrick

I am writing regarding your advertisement in the Guardian dated 29/09/07. Your advert asked that I send a photo. I have attached a photo of my Mum and Dad's cat Whisky. I hope that you enjoy it! I have also attached my CV, and I hope that this letter is counted as a covering letter.

Kind regards

Ian Carpenter

Friday 12th October 2007

A response from Patrick:

```
Hello Ian,

Thank you. We would like to meet Whisky in order
to see if we have a suitable position for him.
Can he travel alone?

Please advice

Thank you

Patrick Meiier
```

Brilliant! Absolutely brilliant. Patrick is head of Global Sales in a Swiss bank, so he must get quite a few emails in his working day. I sent my email last night around 11 and he's responded by 10.06 the following morning (add an hour for the time difference)! This is definitely the best response I've had so far. I need to thank him for taking it all in the right spirit –

```
Dear Patrick

Thank you so much for your response today, it
really did make me laugh. You may have guessed
that I might not be taking this too seriously.
I  have  a  project  to  apply  for  every  job  in
```

the Guardian newspaper on the 29/9/07. Please
see the following link: http://guardianwork.
blogspot.com. I hope this gives you some idea of
what I am doing. Coincidentally, I am in Geneva
on the weekend of the 27th of October. If you
have looked at my CV, and would like to have a
beer somewhere, it would be very funny to have
a meeting.

Kind regards

Ian Carpenter and Whisky

Around three weeks ago, a couple of friends of ours had
the idea of going to Chamonix for the weekend. I agreed
before I saw the Viaduct des Egratz that leads up into the
mountains (remember, I'm not good with heights). So I
think I may be staying in Geneva on the Saturday night.
Anyway, after all that excitement I also received this from
the British Ecological Society:

Many thanks for your email.

I will be out of the office until the 15th October.
If your query is urgent please call the office on
0208 871 9797.

Kindest Regards

Hannah

And this from the Health Professions Council:

Dear Mr Carpenter,

Please find attached the job description for the
Lead Case Manager role. (See attached file: Lead
Case Manager Jul 07.doc)

Kind regards,

Sam Ha

Human Resources Team Administrator

OK, on to page three, which looks a lot more inviting
than the previous pages – the adverts are large ones, so
they shouldn't take too long to get through. Theatre
Royal Plymouth are looking for an Education Manager, a
Community Engagement Manager, and a Young People's
Programme Director –

Dear Jane

Thank you for your advertisement in the Guardian
dated 29/09/07. I would like to apply for your
positions advertised. I am passionate about the
theatre and the community,

Kind regards

Ian Carpenter

Sunday 14th October 2007

I woke up this morning with blue lip disease. Don't panic, dear reader, this was due to the fact that I had celebrated a fantastic victory for the England rugby team over France in the world cup semi final with a bottle of Des Trois Seigneurs, vin de pays L'aude. That's ironic, Alanis Morissette. England 14 – France 9, and what a game! I wondered how many times I'd need to go round the M25 to get such a score in the Norbert Dentressangle v Eddie Stobart game.

The landline telephone in my house is in the lounge. As discussed earlier, I only smoke in my dining room, therefore I spend the majority of my time at home in there with my spider friend. I rarely go into the lounge. This means that I check the answerphone messages about once a month. This is not good for urgent matters, I agree, and I apologise to any friends who might still be waiting for me to return their calls. However, yesterday, I checked my messages and heard the dulcet tones of Lesley-Anne Ryan from tenUK! She would like me to call her to discuss my application further. Are these people mad?! They want to discuss me being their Marketing Operations Manager? Well I will have to call them tomorrow at lunchtime. I'm slightly nervous about this. I don't know what I'm going to say, but we will see what happens. I see it going a bit like this –

Lesley-Anne: Hello tenUK, Lesley Speaking, how may I help you?

Me: Hello, I'm just returning your voice mail message, my name is Ian Carpenter, and I've applied for your jobs advertised in the Guardian.

Lesley-Anne: (papers rustling in the background) Oh yes, which job where you applying for? It was not clear from your email.

Me: All of them.

Lesley-Anne: But the jobs are very different – Marketing Operations Manager, Operations Director, and Analytics Manager are very different roles. Do you have any experience in any of these areas?

Me: No, sorry.

Lesley-Anne: Could you please stop wasting my time?

Me: Yes. Sorry. Bye-bye.

I will let you know how it all turns out tomorrow evening. Next job:

Can you sell Manchester as a World-Class city region?

I don't know, can you? Not wanting to get all Ross Noble about it, I had images of actually selling Manchester as an object. You know when you have to move a piece of turf on your lawn, you kind of edge it with one of those crescent shaped lawn edgers and scoop it up with a spade? I had an image of going around the outskirts of Manchester (this might take a while) with said lawn edger and literally picking Manchester up. And then selling it. This would need some quite heavy lifting gear, I would imagine... I'll apply tomorrow.

Monday 15th October 2007

I was really excited this morning. Up till this point, the whole enterprise has been rather anonymous – sending emails and receiving responses while hiding behind a computer. Today was going to be my first human, verbal interaction! I had to call Lesley-Anne from tenUK to discuss my application further. I was actually quite nervous about the whole affair. Admittedly, I didn't actually want their job, but I got the same feelings of nervousness as if I was applying for a job normally. I'd planned to do it at work at lunchtime. It would have helped if I'd remembered to bring the telephone number in with me.

After driving home to get the number from the answer machine in my lunchbreak, I psyched myself up to take the plunge. Breathe in for five, and out for seven –

Voicemail. Apparently Lesley is busy and will return my call when she's available.

I didn't hear back from her today. Hopefully I can discuss my application with her tomorrow. Anyway, the Manchester Job –

Dear Kirsty

Can I sell Manchester? Yes I can!!! Please find

attached my CV for your perusal.

Kind regards

Ian Carpenter

This next one is something I shouldn't really talk about (as I was later warned): an organisation that relates to illegal money lending is looking for project managers. What? They're using a catchy but cryptic acronym. Hmmm, let's see – they have secured funding to combat illegal money laundering around London. This looks slightly dangerous to me, but I have worked in a bank... I can do this. OK –

Dear XXXX *[reason for censorship will become clear. Ed.]*

I noted with interest your vacancies advertised in The Guardian dated 29/9/07. As you can see from my attached CV, I worked in a bank for ten years. I know what you mean about laundered money: some people used to bring in ten pound notes that they had left in their pockets when they washed their jeans. We were unable to use them again. I hope that you will consider me for your positions.

Kind regards

Ian Carpenter

Oh, pants –

Dear XXXX

I forgot to attach my CV

Kind regards

Ian Carpenter

This is becoming a habit now, and I think it may be costing me job interviews. Next one: Cirque du Soleil!!! They're looking for people to work in rigging, automation, stage carpentry and electrics in Macau in Asia! How fantastic? They offer a full 18 days paid time off a year, and the interviews are taking place in New York and London. I hope they pay the travel expenses –

Dear Madam/Sir

I read with a considerable amount of interest that you are looking for rigging, automation, stage carpentry, and electrics for your Venetian resort in Macau. I cannot pretend to have any experience in these areas, but I would like to apply for the positions anyway. After all, Carpenter by name, carpenter by nature!!! Please find attached my CV for your perusal.

Kind regards

Ian Carpenter

Anyway, the smoking spider is back tonight. Note to self: I'll need to check if the council will accept tiny, empty spider medicine bottles – she must be storing them down the back of the picture rail somewhere.

Tuesday 16th October 2007

Dear Mr Carpenter,

Thank you for showing an interest in applying to
HCCT. All the information regarding the recruitment
as well as an outline of our services etc. can
be found on our website: www.hcct.org.uk, if you
have any further questions please do not hesitate
contacting me or applying through recruitment
email address. I appologise for a delay in getting
back to you, it was due to the technical problems
that we ahve been experiencing with our emails.

Yours Sincerely

Orkhan Ahmadov
Admin/Finance Officer

As explained above, I will not be taking this application
further. This is a well-meaning charity and I cannot waste
any of their time. They have been experiencing problems
with their emails, and I recommend that anyone who
feels generous should contribute towards their fund.
Their email problem is bad. It has caused them to misspell
apologise and have. I was also disappointed to receive a
rejection for the money-laundering job. Alright, maybe
not as disappointed as when I discovered that the Elgin
Marbles where not actually marbles like the ones we

used to play with in school, but I was disappointed. It seems I had lost concentration and had not read their advertisement correctly –

Dear XXXX

Thank you for your email. I apologise that I got the wrong end of the stick about your job advertisement. However, I can tell you that people really did bring notes into the bank after they had been through the laundry. We used to have to fill in a form, staple it to the note and send it to the bank's bankers. I did have experience of lending money in my ten years at the bank. Admittedly, it was all above board and there was nothing illegal about it. However, experience is experience. Does this change your recommendation? I look forward to receiving your information pack.

Kind regards

Ian Carpenter

I had a conversation with one of my contractors at work today. I was explaining my little project to him. In passing, he mentioned a particular vacancy that had come up since yesterday: the position of leader of the Liberal Democrats! OK, I know this job was not advertised in the Guardian dated 29/09/07, but how could I resist this challenge? Sir Menzies Campbell has resigned and there is a vacancy. I could have this one as a bonus job. A little extra. A bit like having cream on ice cream. I found his resignation letter reproduced on the party's site:

The President

The Liberal Democrats

15th October 2007

When I was elected Leader of the Party in March 2006 I had three objectives. First, to restore stability and purpose in the party following my predecessor's resignation and the leadership campaign itself, second to make the internal operations of the party more professional, and third to prepare the party for a General Election. With the help of others, I believe that I have fulfilled these objectives, although I am convinced that the internal structures of the party need radical revision if we are to compete effectively against Labour and the Conservatives.

But it has become clear that following the Prime Minister's decision not to hold an election, questions about leadership are getting in the way of further progress by the party.

Accordingly I now submit my resignation as Leader with immediate effect.

I do not intend to hold a press conference or to make any further comment.

Yours sincerely,

Menzies Campbell
Leader, Liberal Democrats

Short, succint – I think he's probably an honourable chap. There are no direct links to any vacancies on the site but there is a 'contact us' email address –

Dear Madam/Sir

I have noticed from reading articles in the newspapers, watching the television, and listening to the radio, that you currently have a vacancy for the Leader of your organisation. I would like to apply for the position. I am not a member of your party, but I don't think this should come between us. I have seen representatives from your party on the television, and they all seem like fairly nice people. I would really like to work with them. I understand from the articles in the press that it is a two horse race between Nick Clegg and Duncan Huhne. This would be really boring, so I would like to throw my hat into the ring. I was listening to an article on BBC radio Five Live Drive on my way home from work this evening. Messrs Clegg and Huhne were both on. It seems that the main thread in your thinking at the moment is redistribution of wealth, and social mobility. I would like to deal with each of these issues in order:

Redistribution of wealth. I really believe that this is an important area for the party to be moving in. I am not calling myself wealthy, but I do have three bank accounts. I regularly have to redistribute wealth between these accounts. I use all facilities of the bank. I sometimes call into my local branch. I also telephone them, and even use the internet to transfer funds between my accounts. Did you know that you can even do it via the television?

Social Mobility. Again, this is a most important area for you to be looking at. I would like to socially move from being a Property Manager in Basildon, to being Leader of your party. What better a demonstration of your commitment to Social Mobility? I will not go into any comment on ageism at this current time, as it is probably a sensitive subject in your organisation. I have attached my CV for your perusal, and I would welcome a reply at your earliest convenience.

Could you please explain the job application process in more detail?

Kind regards

Ian Carpenter

So all of that excitement has meant that I have not applied to any more jobs in the Guardian today. I have still not heard back from tenUK: No wonder they need an operations manager, I left my message yesterday and still no reply!!! And Patrick Meiier has not responded to my invitation for a beer in Geneva next weekend. Perhaps he really did just want to meet Whisky.

Wednesday 17th October 2007

My car's got one of those on-board computer things that can measure your fuel consumption over a given journey, or your average speed. I set it to zero on the way in to work today to see how fast I travel on the A127 – an average of 14 mph. Well done the South East. No response from the Liberal Democrats today. They must have a lot on their minds. And still no response from my voice mail message to tenUK. I did, however, receive an email from the aforementioned shadowy acronym at war with illegal money lending, thanking me for my enquiry. It included several attachments containing information about them and their project, a job profile and instructions on how to apply. They also asked that I avoid passing on any details of this 'covert opperation' to anyone outside the 'enforcement community'! I have to admit I am a bit scared by this. It's already on my blog!!! I've now edited the relevant blog entry *[which explains earlier censored name. Related material further amended in this book. Ed.]*, so I should be ok. I hope. I have to think about the welfare of my cats Lenny and Hippy. I can *not* get caught up in any covert operations. I haven't even opened the attachments to the email. I know nothing. I should have just left it with the rejection email instead of pushing it further. Anyway, for the sake of Lenny and Hippy, I had to send an immediate withdrawal –

Dear XXXX

I withdraw my application for your job. It all
sounds a bit cloak and dagger to me.

Thanks anyway.

Ian Carpenter

PS You work late don't you?

This is true – the email was received at 9.30 last night.
So on to the next job: oh no, it's the NHS again!!! I've
already been rejected by their computer once, can it
happen again? I'm not holding out much hope. They want
a Director of Human Resources... phew – closing date
17th October! Again, they're directing me to a website.
The computer says 'no' to me on these things, but there
is an email address –

Dear Lynne

I am writing following your recent advertisement
for Director of Human Resources. I was relieved to
see that the closing date was today, and I have
just managed to apply on time. Your advertisement
directed me towards your website www.jobs.nhs.
uk. I would not like to apply for your position
through this route. I recently applied to the NHS
on the 30th September for a Gateway to Leadership

Programme. I was declined by your automated screening service, before a human being got to look at my application! So therefore, I would like to apply in the (new fashioned) old fashioned way, by attaching my CV for your perusal. Should you have any queries, please do not hesitate to contact me.

Kind regards

Ian Carpenter

End of page three!!! Well, apart from an advert for guardianjobs.co.uk, and I am already registered. It is odd though, I haven't had an email from them in two months but today I received an email for a job. Are they trying to challenge me? Onwards. Page four looks just as inviting as page three: Pilgrims are looking for an 'Operations Manager (Operational Consultancy)', an 'Operations Manager (Consultancy)' — no idea what the difference might be — and a 'Training Manager':

Pilgrims is one of the UK's leading security risk management companies, providing a range of specialist consultancy, operational and information services to a significant blue chip client base around the globe.

Well done you. Well they must be specialists if they have to differentiate between Operational Consultancy and

Consultancy. No closing date, just send a CV. OK –

Dear Madam/Sir

I am writing following your three job advertisements
in the Guardian dated 29/9/07. The Operations
Manager (Operational Consultancy) role appeals to
me. It asks for experience of working in hostile
environments and within a commercial organisation.
I often work in hostile environments. For example,
I was washing up this evening while my two cats
(Hippy and Lenny) were fighting over the Iams.
The Operations Manager (Consultancy) role also
appeals to me. I have to be honest, I was a
bit unsure about the need to undertake impact
analysis. Does this hurt? Are we provided with
protective equipment? Of all your three positions,
Training Manager seems about the most suited
to me. I have attached my CV for your perusal.
Should you have any further queries, please do
not hesitate to contact me.

Kind regards

Ian Carpenter

Thursday 18th October 2007

Dear Ian,

BES Policy Officer Vacancy

Thank you for taking the time to apply for the Policy Officer position at the British Ecological Society. The BES received a large number of applications for this position from qualified individuals. The selection panel has decided not to short list you for an interview on this occasion, as there were candidates who better met our key requirements. The decision was arrived at by assessing how the candidates met the advertised job specifications. I wish you the best of luck in your career development.

Kindest regards

Hannah

Clerical Officer, British Ecological Society

I applied for this position on the 11th October and I was slightly late in applying. If you remember, the vacancy had closed at noon and I applied late in the evening. I think they must have appointed someone that afternoon. Hannah sends her kindest regards, so she seems like a friendly person –

Dear Hannah

Thank you for your email. I am obviously disappointed, but not as disappointed as I was when I found out that the Elgin Marbles were not actually marbles like the ones you played with at school! Could you just tell me, was it because I missed the deadline of noon? Did you make your decision that afternoon? Thank you for your best wishes in my future career development. I am currently applying for quite a number of jobs, and I am sure one will lead somewhere interesting.

Kind regards

Ian Carpenter

I also received this from my Arch Nemesis, the NHS:

Dear Ian

Thank you for your interest in this post. All applicants must complete our standard application form, either online or by submitting a paper copy. We cannot accept CVs. I have tried to call you at home but there is no answer and I could not see a mobile number on your CV or email. Please contact me if you receive my email this morning and we can arrange for your to complete our standard application form. However, I am afraid this post

closed at midnight last night and we must get the
final applications on our system this morning. I
therefore could not accept an application from
you after midday today.

Kind regards,

Sarah Barnett

Project Co-ordinator

Blimey, how hard is it to get a job at the NHS?!? Firstly,
they have more typos than The Guardian itself. In my first
application to them, they spelt application, appliction, and
now it's 'and we can arrange for your to complete our
standard application form'! Who is 'your'? Is this someone
that works in their offices transcribing application forms?
Imagine a conversation in the NHS office –

Sarah Barnett: Hello, your, we have someone here that has
sent a CV, but doesn't want to fill in an application form
online. Can you fill the form out for him?

your: yes, no problem at all.

Alright –

Dear Sarah

Thank you for your email. Sadly, it looks as if I

have missed the boat on this occasion. Thank you for trying to call me today and you are right, I was not at home, as I was working in my office in Basildon. As you will recall from my original email, I do not trust the online application process; I was rejected within five minutes on a Sunday morning! I hope that today was not too manic for you, what with having to get all those applications on by noon. You can get that repetitive strain injury from too much typing you know! Anyway, it was nice to hear from you, and should you not find a suitable candidate, would you please email me and perhaps I could fill in an application form.

Kind regards

Ian Carpenter

Administration over, on to the next job: 'Do you want an international career?' Erm, not really. 'If you would like the challenge of working for a vibrant international company, then polish your CV and apply directly to job. london@meltwaternews.com.' Ok, here goes —

Dear Madam/Sir

I saw your advertisement for the above position advertised in the Guardian dated 29/09/07. You have requested that I polish my CV, and why not? We are all one Europe now! Unfortunately, my computer skills are not such that I could fit a flag of Poland on my CV. I have therefore attached a picture of the Polish flag in my email. I hope that this counts. I look forward to hearing from you soon.

Kind regards

Ian Carpenter

Saturday 20th October 2007

This morning I woke up with swollen tonsils, due to too much snoring due to that bottle of merlot in the restaurant, the food of which I can still smell on my fingers, and 'a dull ache in my forehead disease'.

My parents live in the Forest of Dean in Gloucestershire. According to Google maps, a distance of 185 miles or 3 hours 31 minutes distance. They run a traditional rural shop, where people put a paper order in for the whole week and Mrs Jones has a bloomer on Thursday – you get the idea. I don't see them very often due to the distance between us. We are the archetypal non-nuclear family. It's my mum's birthday next week, so it was decided she should come down for a weekend visit to celebrate the passing of another year. My dad drove her and a close family friend Phyllis down and they arrived at around 1pm yesterday (I'd taken the afternoon off). My dad was just dropping the two of them off, as he couldn't get anyone to look after the shop for the weekend – a journey of 370 miles, and a size 12 carbon wellington boot-print (and, yes, my mum can drive, and, no, I do not know why she didn't drive herself). We all drove straight to a bar on Southend seafront for the afternoon – it was one of those great autumnal afternoons where you get crisp, shiny sunshine – then we booked my mum and Phyllis into a local hotel (in case you think I am not hospitable; I do not have a spare bedroom. I turned it into a study when I went back to university). When we unloaded the car, I discovered that they'd brought their own toaster, bread, and margarine, which they proceeded to arrange neatly on the sideboard of their shared twin room. I suppose they must have thought we may not have learned how to toast bread here in Essex. Anyway, after dad had left and Nicky had returned from work, we went for a meal in the restaurant, the food of which I could smell on my fingers this morning.

As you might have guessed, I didn't do any work on my little project yesterday. I think the Guardian Job Gods can sense that I haven't done any work, as I haven't received any emails at all, which is a bit of a bonus as it means I can crack on with applying for the jobs.

Saturday 20th October 2007

The Guardian JobMatch team have identified an opportunity that may be of interest to you. The advertiser is UNITED UTILITIES LTD and the title of the vacancy they are advertising is Business Development Manager x3. To find out more please click here: http://jobs.guardian.co.uk/ job/297903/business-development-manager-x3/?grs e=grse 1&email=jobmatch&licampaignid=300601

Kind Regards

The Guardian Jobs Team

To Unsubscribe, please log in to Guardian Jobs and delete saved searches. To Log in, click here: http://www.guardianjobs.co.uk/my-details?grse=g rse 1&email=Jobmatch unsub

Now I'm slightly more certain that the Guardian Jobs Team is laying down the gauntlet, as it were. I may be being paranoid, but the way they've signed off 'with kind regards' makes me suspicious. Once more unto the breach, Guardian Jobs Team, I cannot refuse your challenge –

Job: Business Development Manager x3, UNITED UTILITIES LTD

Shouldn't that be 'Jobs'? Ah well, this *is* the Guardian –

Thank you for applying for the position of :

Business Development Manager x3.

App. Source : **GuardianJobs**

Posting Ref : **ADV330215GU5**

If you would like to view the job advert, please <u>click here</u>

Thank you, I will

Applying for this job should only take a few minutes. Fill in the Personal Details form making sure that your email address and phone numbers are up to date. Then upload any documents requested e.g. CV. When your application is complete you will receive an acknowledgement by email for your records. Your application is then ready to be considered for shortlisting.

When you are ready to begin your application click "Next "

OK, I've filled in my personal details and uploaded my CV. There. That was easy. I still don't trust the online application process though, so I'll expect to be declined within a couple of minutes. OK, next:

With a name like Guinness you might think our brand was pretty good already.

Fantastic! A job working for Guinness!

Today we have no connection with the brewery, but we're proud of our heritage and keen to build on our reputation as one of the country's largest providers of housing.

Oh pants.

Sunday 21st October 2007

From Guinness:

This position is now closed and no late applications will be received.

Fair enough. And The Prostate Cancer Charity will not receive an application from me for their Volunteer Development Manager, even though they do welcome applications from all sections of the community. Ditto the Petsavers Fundraiser, though the position was based in Gloucester, which would have been handy for my mum and dad's shop. Espresso Education are looking for a Business Development Executive, but the closing date was the 19th October 2007. Worth a try –

Dear Madam/Sir

I noticed that you had the above position advertised in The Guardian dated 29/09/07. The closing date was the 19th October 2007. I appreciate that I am late, but I have had my mum visiting with her friend Phyllis over the weekend. Would you still accept my application?

Kind regards

Ian Carpenter

Last one on page four!!! And for the first time since I started my little project, I need stationery – Jigsaw want a 'London Based Visual Merchandise and Stylist' and I have to apply in writing to Faye McLeod. I'm off to buy some stamps and an envelope – oh, and some new ink for the printer...

Whoever sucked the air out of the plastic wrapping on my ink cartridge did a very good job. It took me at least twenty minutes to get it open. The air must have been sucked out by someone with the lung capacity of an Olympic rower. OK, so Jigsaw want people who have a proven track record in fashion visual merchandising. Hmm, tricky one –

```
Faye McLeod
Visual Director
Jigsaw
21st October 2007
Re: Visual Merchandisers & stylists

Dear Ms McLeod

I am writing following your recent advertisement
for the above position. Although, I do not have
any direct experience in this area, I do select
the appropriate tie for my shirt every morning. I
would like to think that I rarely make a fashion
faux pas. I would hope that the people at work
would tell me if I did. I also do my own hair (with
full use of the mirror in the dining room) every
```

morning. I did not used to use any products on my hair, but recently I have been taken to using a styling wax by VO5; it is very good. I have taken a picture of the styling wax to prove that I use it. You will notice from the picture that there is one of those funny orb things above the pot. I don't know what this means, but I think it may mean that this was meant to be the job for me. Please find attached Curriculum Vitae, and picture with the funny orb thingy on it. I look forward to hearing from you soon.

Kind regards

Ian Carpenter

Monday 22nd October 2007

I went to work this morning knowing that mum and Phyllis were being picked up by my dad to be driven home again – if you're going to make a carbon wellington boot-print, you may as well make a pair. Although it's nice to have your family over, I was really looking forward to getting back to normal and sitting on the bus with Lenny. This might require an explanation: Lenny has already been mentioned above. He's one of my two cats. Lenny's had a troubled life. He joined our little family during a period when my partner was working in a pet shop. He was the last cat left over from a litter of kittens. I don't think anyone liked him because he has a funny squidge on his face that makes him look like he's laughing. And because he was the last kitten left, he spent rather too much time with the birds in the pet shop and now every time he sees a bird, he has to make a bird-like squawking sound. This has gradually developed into a general anxiety disorder. He always has to come in through the dining room doors even if the kitchen door is open and he hates carrier bags rustling to the extent that he will jump about four feet in the air if he encounters one. Anyway, as explained before, at home I spend a great deal of my time in the dining room. I sit on a dining chair, and Lenny likes me to pull up another dining chair alongside mine. He will then just sit there on his dining chair next to me, and it sort of feels as though we're sitting together on the top deck of a double-decker bus. Hence the expression 'to sit on the bus with Lenny'. I use it now to mean 'getting back to normal after you've been on holiday, or had visiting family disrupting your usual routine'.

Tonight the smoking spider decided to sit on the bus with me and Lenny. She didn't make an appearance for the whole weekend with mum and Phyllis around, but she's back now they're gone.

Today I spoke to a human being from tenUK!!! You'll recall that they'd left a message on my answerphone around ten days ago and I'd returned their call but got a voicemail message. Well, today they called again. It went like this:

Kerri: Hello is that Ian.

Me: Yes, who's calling?

Kerri: It is Kerri from tenUK, you have left us an answerphone message?

Me: Yes, I was returning your call, you said that you wanted to discuss my application further.

Kerri: Which job did you apply for?

(Hmm, tricky, I have applied for quite a few recently)

Me: I think it was for Operations Manager.

Kerri: Oh, Ops Manager, we have had loads of entrants for that, we have a pile of CVs which we are sifting through.

Me: So what was it that you wanted to discuss?

Kerri: Oh nothing, I was just returning your answerphone message.

Me: So is there some kind of Application Process?

Kerri: Oh yes, we will sift through the CVs and you may be selected for a telephone interview.

Me: So I shall expect to hear from you?

Kerri: Yes within the next few days.

Me: Alright then, I'll speak to you soon.

Within ten minutes I received a text message:

Ian we have not received a CV from you. If you would like to apply for a role, please email this to HR@TenUK. com.

WHAT?!?! They received my email on the 9th October 2007 enclosing a CV. They must have had it – how else did they leave me a message on my answerphone? –

Dear Ten

I am writing following our telephone conversation,

and a subsequent text message. You have had my CV. Please find attached a copy of my original email. I would still love to be part of your revolution!

Kind regards

Ian Carpenter

So, two weeks on and we are back to square one. Hello? –

We thank you for your interest in tenUk and will be in touch shortly.

Kind regards,

HR at tenUK

Oh, I'm sure they will. OK, here's another email:

Strictly Confidential-
Addressee Only
RE - Application for Coaching Consultant - UK Sport

Dear Ian,

Further to your application to the above post, I write to inform you that regrettably, on this occasion, you were unsuccessful. May I take this opportunity to thank you for your interest in the role and please do not let this deter you from applying for future jobs within UK Sport.

Yours sincerely

Danni Thomas
Human Resources Administrator

OK, I won't be deterred –

Dear Danni

Thank you for your email. However, I was really disappointed by your rejection of my application. I really do like watching elite sport. Only last weekend, I watched England be beaten by South Africa in the World Cup Final. I also watched Lewis Hamilton fail to win the F1 Championship. Would you please reconsider my application?

Kind regards

And, finally, this from the Lib Dems!:

Dear Ian

Many thanks for your email, the contents of which have been noted. You have to already be a Member of Parliament in order to stand for Leader of the Party, however, thank you for your application and for writing in.

```
Best wishes

Emma Peall

Information Co-ordinator
```

Well you can't argue with that... Or can you?

Tuesday 23rd October 2007

Dear Emma

Thank you for your email, I am glad that you have noted the contents of my email. I, in turn, note the contents of your email. I notice that nominations close for leader on the 31st October 2007. Do you think it is possible to become a Member of Parliament by then? Are there any seats going spare at the moment? I appreciate that I may miss the deadline this time around. However, for future reference, how do I go about becoming an MP? Do you have a leaflet that you could send me? I look forward to your reply.

Kind regards

Ian Carpenter

I spent the day travelling to a property just south of Heathrow Airport. The journey there was broken up by a close game of the Norbert Dentressangle v Eddie Stobart Game. Norbert went into the lead around junction 26 of the M25 then I spotted an Eddie around junction 16 making it 1-1 but Eddie finally pipped it at the death when I spotted another of his lorries just after Junction 15. Final score: France 1: England 2.

When I got home I found a message on my answerphone from Lesley-Anne at tenUK. She would like to invite me for a telephone interview. Now, P G Wodehouse style, let us just sum up what's happened so far with these people:

1. I sent a CV by email.

2. They left a message on my home phone, asking to discuss the application further.

3. I left a message for them with my mobile telephone number.

4. They called me back asking what I wanted.

5. I receive a text message indicating they do not have my CV.

6. I send my CV in to them again.

7. They called my home phone again and left a message saying they'd like to discuss my application further, and inviting me for a telephone interview.

No wonder they need an Operations Director! So far, their operations have not been directed very well at all. Oh well, I'll call them tomorrow lunchtime. Administration over, on with the jobs – ActionAid will also accept applications from all aspects of the community. No, I don't think so. What's this? 'Home help required by Female Writer in Notting Hill Gate':

Housework, shopping and whatever comes up. Over-qualified people welcomed. A sense of humour helps and you'll need to be reliable, practical, keenly helpful and able to commit to a minimum of six months. Email (no attachments please) with brief résumé and full contact details.

This advert looks sublimely ridiculous beneath the advert for the international charity. Part of me wants to leave this writer with their over-qualified shopper. However, I really can't resist –

Dear Madam

I read with interest your advertisement in the Guardian dated 29/9/07. I am overqualified and I have a sense of humour, for example: What do you call a three-legged donkey? A Wonkey. I look forward to your earliest response.

Kind regards

Ian Carpenter

The next advert is for a fellowship at Harvard University.

Applications must come from the candidate's university. As I am not currently studying, I will be unable to apply. However, I am pleased to hear the fellowship provides a stipend of $20,500. Foundling Museum = charity = no. Some media company require professionals with one year's B2B or B2C phone sales experience. They want applicants to call, so I'll add them to tomorrow's lunchtime calls list. The Future Laboratory's job closed on the 8th October, which is a terrible shame because:

Ours is not a 9-5 environment. Commitment, enthusiasm and passion are essential. Attractive package includes Christmas office closure, pension scheme, all of the food and drink you can manage, the office dog to walk and company performance related bonus.

Great incentives, but funny that shutting the office at Christmas comes top of their list.

Wednesday 24th October 2007

I called tenUK again at lunchtime today and guess what? Voicemail. However I was heartened to receive the following email:

Dear Ian

Thank you for your email. Our selection process looks into the competencies identified by the job description. Unfortunately in this instance you did not satisfy the level of experience in this field required for the job role and therefore we cannot reconsider your application.

Kind Regards

Danni Thomas
Human Resources Administrator
UK Sport

So, they're not prepared to reconsider. Never mind. No real news from anyone today. I was looking forward to hearing from the female writer in Notting Hill. Perhaps my three-legged wonky donkey joke is not really that funny. But I *do* have some news – my spider has a suitor! There's been another spider in the corner of the room. I'm not sure if the two of them are lovers, but the suitor-spider has been hanging around my little nicotine-loving arachnid for two days now. I don't know a lot about spider mating rituals, but this guy's been checking her out from several angles while keeping a distance of around two feet away. Maybe I'm learning something about nature and overcoming my fear of spiders. Maybe I should, instead, be learning to dust away the spiders' cobwebs? Anyway, on with the jobs: the Financial Times are looking for a Marketing Executive. 'To apply send your CV to jobs@FT.com quoting reference MexecIF.' What? No covering letter or anything? OK –

Dear Madam/Sir

I quote MexecIF.

Kind regards

Ian Carpenter

They also have positions for 'SUB-EDITORS'. This must be important, as the job title is all in capitals –

Dear Charlotte

I read with the utmost interest your advertisement for SUB EDITOR in the Guardian dated 29/09/07. Why is the job title in capital letters? I would like to apply, and have attached my CV.

Kind regards

IAN CARPENTER

The CAPITAL LETTER DISEASE is contagious on this page. According to Complimentry Art Gallery, 'Candidates Must be Efficient, Loyal, Honest, and Dedicated' –

Dear Madam/Sir

I am writing regarding your advertisement in the Guardian dated 29/09/07. I am Efficient, Loyal, Honest, and Dedicated. I have attached my CV, and I look forward to your earliest response.

Kind regards

Ian Carpenter

Next: SKIrecruit. I'll come back to that one... Hmmm. I'm going to the Swiss Alps this weekend. I'm not sure it's a great idea, because I'm not at all good with heights. I'm concerned about this Viaduc des Egratz. That looks like a very high bridge to me... Perhaps tomorrow I'll send another email to Mr Meiier.

Thursday 25th October 2007

COMPLEMENTRY ART GALLERY121 LEDYARD AVE.
BU& FFALO,
NY,14043
NEW YORK.
Phone #: 773-878-4770

Hello Ian Carpenter,

Am Ryan Gray from COMPLEMENTRY ART
GALLERIES . We are glad to offer you a job position
with our company. We need someone to work for the
company as a Account Manager,Representative/Book
keeper in England . This is in view of our not
having a major office presently in the England .You
don't need to have an Office and this certainly
won't disturb any form of work you have going at
the moment.

We source the following variety of clothing
materials:-batiks, assorted fabrics for interior
decor, silk and traditional costumes which we have
clients we supply weekly in the England .Presently
with the amount of Orders we have, we cannot put them
on hold for fear of loosing the customers outrightly.
It's a known fact,that it's not easy to start a
business in a new market (being the England).
There are hundreds of competitors, close direct

contacts between suppliers and customers and other difficulties,which impede our sales promotion.We have decided to deliver the products upfront, it's very risky but it would push up sales by 25 percent. Unfortunately we are unable to open Bank Accounts in England without first registering the company name.

Secondly we cannot cash these payments from the England soon enough, as international Cheques take about 15-20 working days for cash to be made available.We lose about 75,000 USD of net income each month because we have money transfer delays.Your task is to coordinate payments from customers and help us with the payment process. You are not involved in any sales or marketing. Once orders are received and sorted we deliver the product to a customer.The customer receives and checks the products.

After this has been done the customer has to pay for the products.About 90 percent of our customers prefer to pay through Certified Cheque so We decided to open this new job position for solving this problem.Your tasks are:

1. Receive payment from Customers.

2. Cash Payments at your Bank (Upon my instruction).

3. Deduct 300 pounds which will be your commission/ pay on each Payment processed.

4. Forward balance after deduction of commission/ pay to any of the offices you will be contacted to send payment to.(Payment is to forwarded either by MoneyGram or Western Union Money Transfer Preferably).

But the problem we have is trust, But we have our way of getting anyone that gets away with our money, I mean the IRS and Secret Service branch in Washington gets involve. Our payments will be issued out in your name and you can have them cashed at your bank or other Cashing Services.Deduct your commission and forward the balance to the company . If you are interested, N: B, Please send to me the listed information below:

#Your full name:
#Your full home address,
#Your age as well your marital status and your gender
#direct contact telephone number:
#Nationality.

Thanks for your anticipated action and we hope to hear back from you.

Ryan Gray
COMPLEMENTRY ART GALLERIES.

Oh pants.

I reckon this may be a scam, and I've sent them my CV. This contains my name, address, telephone number, and date of birth. I spend several hours every week shredding all the pointless letters I receive, so as not to be scammed. And I've gone and emailed these people my personal details. Well done me. I can now look forward to a life of constantly checking credit reference agencies to see if I've funded some drug trafficking/money laundering operation. Well I'm certainly going to email the Guardian. Do they not vet their adverts? I thought the female writer in Notting Hill was a bit weird, but this one goes well beyond weird –

Dear Madam/Sir

I recently applied for a job in the Guardian dated 29/09/07. It was on page 9, towards the bottom of the paper. I have attached a picture of the job advertisement. As you can see, it appears to be some sort of money laundering scheme. I am slightly concerned about this. I thought that the Guardian was a reputable newspaper and would not have anything to do with such schemes. Could

you please reassure me that if I apply for any
jobs in the future, it will not be for anything
illegal? Could you please respond by return of
email?

Kind regards

Ian Carpenter

Today at work I decided to leave another message on the
voicemail of tenUK. When I got home I found another
email from them:

Hi Ian

As you can imagine we have been very busy managing
applications for posts advertised and it has
therefore proved difficult to speak when you have
called in of late. If you would please confirm
which role you are applying for?

Many thanks in advance

Hannah

Fantastic! —

Dear Hannah

Thank you for your email. We always seem to
miss each other. I would like to apply for all

three positions advertised in the Guardian dated 29/09/07. The positions advertised were:

Operations Director

Marketing Operations Manager

Analytics Manager

Lesley-Anne called on the 23rd October 2007 inviting me to a telephone interview. I am not sure which position I had been short-listed for. Please do not hesitate to contact me on my mobile number. I look forward to hearing from you soon.

Kind regards

Ian Carpenter

And here's one from The Guardian:

Thank you for your letter to the Guardian. Unless you have indicated otherwise, it will be considered for publication - as long as you have included the following details:

(1) A full name and full postal address (including street, town and county);

(2) A daytime contact telephone number. It is also helpful to include a reference (headline, section, publication date) to the article to which your

letter refers. Letters are usually published with only a village, town or city as the address (or an organisation where relevant). The other contact details are for verification only. If your email did not include them, please resend the full text of your letter with these details to letters@ guardian.co.uk. Do NOT reply to this automatically generated email as the account from which it is sent cannot accept incoming email. Whether or not we publish your letter, it will be read and forwarded, where appropriate, to the relevant journalist or section editor. Please note that letters may be edited.

Regards

Letters editor
The Guardian

OK. We'll just have to wait and see what happens.

Friday 26th October 2007

I have to admit that I am a little bit scared tonight. The Viaduc des Egratz has been playing on my mind all day. We're off to Chamonix tomorrow. 'We' being my friend Lez, Liz (Lez's girlfriend), Nicky and me. Why would someone who does not like heights go up a mountain? I suppose I see it as a bit of a challenge. Also, I intend on visiting Patrick's offices in Geneva, and hopefully I'll be able to take a photo of us together for the blog. The trip will mean I'll be unable to apply for any jobs this weekend... unless, of course, I bring my paper with me to Switzerland and apply from there... But what if there's some kind of soft drink spillage in the hand luggage? Hmmm. They do have computers in Switzerland, as was demonstrated by Patrick's email about Whisky, so I might be able to send a few emails... The Guardian work supplement dated 29/09/07 has been quite a large part of my life over the past few weeks. I think it deserves a little holiday...

Today at work someone said to me, 'Ian, did you see Martin Jol, the Spurs manager's been sacked? That means there's a vacancy...' Thanks, Laura. This'll be my second transgression into non-Guardian jobs but, considering my recent experience with job ads from the Guardian, I'm glad to be on safe ground – I feel fairly certain Tottenham Hotspur don't want me to launder money for them –

Dear Madam/Sir

I have read, listened to, and watched several articles regarding Martin Jol today. I am still unsure whether he was sacked before, during, or after the game last night. Anyway, that is all immaterial, because I would like to apply for the position of Manager of your Football Club. I am a keen supporter of Liverpool Football Club, but this should not come between us. I also drove by White Hart Lane on the way to a property that I manage in Green Lanes. I liked the look of the area, I felt really comfortable there. I am also a fan of Paul Hawksbee on Talk Sport. He seems like a very nice man, and if that is the type of fan that you have at White Hart Lane, I think it is the place for me. Did you hear the programme when they invented the Norbert Dentressangle v Eddie Stobart Game? I have attached my CV for your perusal, and I look forward to your earliest response.

Kind regards

Ian Carpenter

PS Don't tell my partner, she is a bit of an Arsenal fan!

Anyway, there we go – a second deviation from my Guardian jobs pages but, hey, it *is* coming with me to Switzerland for the weekend.

Monday 29th October 2007

We arrived safely back home last night and it was fantastic to sit on the bus with Lenny. The weekend in Swizerland/France went by so quickly. We flew out of London City Airport, which I must say is absolutely fantastic, at 7.50 a.m. (and, no, this was not too early to have a beer in the bar first). Liz fell asleep on the flight on the way over and this gave Lez an ideal opportunity to play Human Buckaroo. He tried to balance as many free Swiss Air chocolates as he could on Liz's shoulders before she woke up. This kept us entertained for about ten minutes. On landing the first thing we did was set off for the Rue du Rhone, the place of work of Patrick Meiier at ACM. I now understand why he did not agree to meet me for a beer. There are no pubs in Geneva. We spent three hours yesterday afternoon trying to find one. Anyway, this seemed like a perfect photo opportunity for the Guardian jobs pages. We tried to go up to ACM Currency Markets SA, but the lift wouldn't let us up there without some special key code. However, as you can see, l was able to peruse my paper while sitting comfortably in the lovely leather sofa in the foyer of the building:

There were some really important looking people there that gave Lez and I a quizzical look as they made their way to the lift. Nicky and Liz were having nothing to do with all this, and were ambling along outside on Rue du Rhone. They really do sell a lot of posh watches in Geneva. Anyway, to avoid the dreaded Viaduc des Egratz, we decided to take a detour via Evian les Bains. Yes, where the water comes from. Lake Geneva really is spectacular. The water is crystal clear. I regretted not bringing a supply of plastic bottles. I could have filled them up from the lake and flogged them for £1.50 a bottle. I feel I missed out on a pension building opportunity. In the end I wished I'd just bitten the bullet and gone via the Viaduc because the old road up the mountain was absolutely terrifying! Seriously, why do people do this for recreation? The road was one of those winding Swiss/French roads that you see on Top Gear. The drops were phenomenal. I spent the best part of an hour with my eyes shut, and my hands produced a small lake of their own from perspiration. We finally ended up spending a lovely evening in a Fondue Restaurant in Chamonix but the cheesy smell impregnated my new alpine coat – I'll have to get it dry cleaned later this week. Then, yesterday, after a brief walk and some stone-skipping on an alpine lake, we made our way back down the mountain. I took some pictures of the Viaduc, as we passed it on the way back down. Here's one of them:

Just to reiterate: I'm not good with heights. I recommend anyone with a similar fear not to go up a great big mountain.

I've taken the day off work today. I'm going to spend the whole day concentrating on applying for more jobs. It's quite exciting being at the computer during the daytime. Up until now, my little project has happened in the evening. I come in from work, check my emails, maybe send a few. Today I get to hear the 'ding dong' as they arrive in my inbox. 'Ding dong' – there, see?:

Dear Ian

Many thanks for your email and application....

Having carefully reviewed your cv and noted your extensive experience in finance and property management, I regret to inform you that we will not be taking your application further on this occasion. Whilst your experience in your field is of undoubted interest to us, especially your association with Green Lanes (it's extensive Mediterranean and middle eastern cuisine is of great note to all of us at the Lane) I am afraid that we have recently filled our vacant roles. Whilst not a consideration on this occasion, should you wish to make any further applications, I would advise removing all references from those in red from your cv!

I wish you all the best in your future career.

Jonathan Waite
Customer Services Manager
Tottenham Hotspur Football & Athletic Co Ltd
Bill Nicholson Way

Brilliant! I'm pleased that they are familiar with the fine work of the restaurateurs on Green Lanes but I was a bit disappointed that they had not granted me the opportunity of an interview. I understand they have offered the position to Juande Ramos. That'll teach me for having the weekend off. You snooze, you lose. Oh well, this deserves a reply –

Dear Jonathan

Thank you for your quick response to my email that I sent you on Friday evening. I am pleased that you are familiar with the fine work of the restaurateurs on Green Lanes. I never believed all the things that I saw on the Life of Grime television programme. I understand that you have now appointed Juande Ramos. I appreciate that he has more experience in the area of football management, but I would like to see him manage finance or property as well as me! Anyway, thank you once again for your quick response.

Kind regards

Ian Carpenter

Tuesday 30th October 2007

I arrived back at work today with a fairly big bump. It seems all of my properties have leaked water from their various roofs and guttering. That'll teach me for having a weekend off, again. Anyway, one of the gardeners I work with sent me a bizarre email last night. He'd been following the progress of my little project on my blog, and it seems he'd picked up on the orb in my hair wax photograph:

Dear Ian

Well here we are another week over and hopefully you are ok and the bridge did not collapse :) anyway first thing is you still did not send me the email about the work you want done and secondly 0--0-- -0---0---0---0---0---0---0 you thought that your picture of your hair gel was strange with the aura above it........ well for the first time today since i have been back i looked at my pictures from Prauge. we wwere on the Charles Bridge at night and i was taking pictures as you do and i attach a copy of one of them...... This bridge was built in the 13th century so you would expect some stories about ghosts and stuff but take a look at this !!!!!!!!!!!!!!! at the bottom of the picture you can see clearly the skeleton of a ghost and

this has really freaked me out big time and i am
going to bed now as i am downstairs all on my own
!!!!!!!!!! call me and tell me what you think !!!!!
Barry

How bizarre!!! It's Halloween coming up, and I am
definitely not good with ghosts. Anyway, Lenny has been
in the wars whilst we were away on holiday. He must
have had a little fight with another local cat. He has an
abscess on his left ear. I like to call it 'pussy ear that smells
like used dental floss disease'. Have you ever tried to give
antibiotics to a cat with an anxiety disorder? Not easy. OK,
down to business. We've all seen the Liberal Democrats
on the television. They like to talk a bit. Well, dear reader,
you may want to skip the following email that I received
from them today:

Dear Ian,

Thank you for your email which has been forwarded
to me by my colleague Emma Peall. In order to
be elected as a Liberal Democrat MP, you first
need to be selected by a Local Party as the
candidate in their constituency. In order to be
selected you will need to apply for inclusion on
the list of Liberal Democrat Approved Candidates
for the Westminster Parliament. Please note that
in order to be assessed for approval you must
be a fully paid up Party member of at least 12
months standing. We would recommend that all
members seeking approval arrange to pay their
membership fees by direct debit, as any lapse
in membership may affect approval status. You
can contact membership@libdems.org.uk for more
details or join via the following link https://
www.libdems.org.uk/support/join.html?ref=home.

Please find attached the following documents. In order
to maximise your chances of approval it is important
that you take time to read all of these thoroughly
before completing your application form:

1) Candidates' questionnaire

This self-assessment questionnaire is designed to
help you judge whether you are ready to apply for
approval, to highlight the areas upon which you

will be assessed and help identify any competencies where you might benefit from further experience or training.

2) Becoming a PPC – an overview

This outlines the process of approval and selection.

3) Application guidance notes

These contain detailed guidance on how to fill in all sections of the form.

4) Application form – sections A, B & C

This part of the application is forwarded to the assessors before your assessment day. You should return the original and 6 copies of this section of the form in hard copy to the Candidates' Office, and one copy by email to candidates.office@ libdems.org.uk.

5) Application form – section D

This contains important information about sponsors. Each sponsor should be given a copy of this section, along with a sponsorship form and a copy of "Qualities looked for in a effective PPC or PEPC". It is the applicant's responsibility to ensure that 5 signed sponsorship forms are returned to the Candidates' Office with the application form. You should note that your application will not normally be processed until all 5 sponsor forms have been returned.

6) Qualities looked for in an effective PPC or PEPC.

7) Sponsorship form.

8) Application form – sections E, F & G

These sections contain your personal declaration, declaration of interests and medical declaration. Please complete these fully and make sure the final declaration is signed.

9) Application form – sections H & I

Biographical and Monitoring Information.

These sections do not form part of the assessment. The biographical information will be used to provide information about you to the media and general public should you be approved and selected for a constituency. The monitoring information is used internally to assess our diversity policies. It will be used for anonymous statistical analyses which may be made public, but no personal information will be released unless you give your consent as indicated in section H.

10) Contact list of Regional Candidates' Chairs (RCCs)

Your RCC is well placed to offer advice on the approval process, and to help you meet any training or personal development needs you may have. Once you have submitted your form and it has been successfully processed, they will organise an assessment day in your region if possible. Please note that an assessment day can only be organised when there are sufficient candidates. The English Candidates' Committee has agreed as a target that all candidates will be offered an assessment day within 6 months of having submitted their application form. If you have a particular seat in mind, please allow plenty of time before the selection process is scheduled to apply for assessment. Please let the Candidates' Office know if you are willing to travel outside your region for assessment as this may increase your opportunities for assessment.

Completed applications should be returned to the Candidates' Office, along with a deposit cheque for £50 made out to "English Liberal Democrats". This will be returned to you when you have attended an assessment day. In the event of a cancellation less than 4 weeks before the day, this deposit may be retained in order to cover the administrative costs of finding a replacement and you will have to submit another deposit cheque before being offered another day. Unavoidable and sincere reasons for non-attendance will be treated sympathetically.

If you have any questions or queries about the form or application process, please don't hesitate to contact the Candidates' Office on 020 7227 1204.

Tamsin Hewett
English Candidates' Officer

Phew! OK –

Dear Tamsin

Thank you for your email. It seems like it's quite a process becoming an MP! I will peruse the contents of your email and let you know whether this is the right thing for me. I really did appreciate your email. It must have taken you some time to type all of that. I hope you took regular breaks, as you can get RSI from too much typing!

Kind regards

Ian Carpenter

I also received my weekly email from The Guardian:

The Guardian JobMatch team have identified an opportunity that may be of interest to you. The advertiser is IAC and the title of the vacancy they are advertising is Technical Sales Manager. To find out more please click here:

http://jobs.guardian.co.uk/job/303031/
technical-sales-manager/?grse=grse 1&email=jobm
atch&licampaignid=311513

Kind Regards

The Guardian Jobs Team

Let's have a look:

Reporting to the Business Manager you will be responsible for generating new business within the stand alone acoustic door and window team.

'Stand alone acoustic door and window team'?!? Does a door stand alone ever? Usually they're attached to some kind of frame, which is usually attached to a, well, wall. What is an 'acoustic door' anyway? Actually, I think the people next door have an acoustic door – there's a sonic boom when they slam it shut at six o'clock in the morning. Applying for that one is fairly straightforward: I just upload my CV online. OK, another one down.

Question: How many Radians in a semi-circle?

Answer: Pi.

Thank you Jeremy Paxman.

Thursday November 1st 2007

I have not worked on my project for a couple of days. This is not because I've fallen foul of the ghosties in Barry's picture, but rather because I was abducted by a very nasty stomach bug on Wednesday morning. It transported me to a strange world, which was basically my bedroom, with the lights off, and me in a foetal position with serious abdominal pains. The strange bug would lead me to the bathroom at fairly regular intervals to make me do things I did not want to do. Today I went to the doctor, and he told me I had 'some kind of stomach bug'. Thanks Doctor. I don't reckon my doctor and the person who named Blue-Tongue Disease would get on very well. Anyway, he gave me some kind of milky stuff to drink, which I think has worked. Again, it has been proven that the Guardian Jobs gods know when I'm not working: I've had no responses from anyone this evening. So I'd better crack on with it. I now realise what with all of the excitement over Switzerland, and being abducted by the bug, that I haven't applied for a single job in over seven days!!! Well let's get on with it: London Business School are looking for a Development Associate:

'You will manage an international portfolio of 150 top prospects to ensure they are solicited for gifts of £50k-£2m for institutional priorities.'

Hmm, I have already had someone soliciting my details through this newspaper, so I'm a bit wary, but –

Dear Madam/Sir

I read with more than a considerable amount of interest your advertisement in the Guardian dated 29/09/07. I was particularly interested in your excellent recreational facilities, including on-site swimming pool, spa pool, sauna, and fully equipped gym. I have recently applied for another job in the Guardian dated 29/09/07, and was led up the garden path. I hope that your request for me to solicit money from an international portfolio is all legitimate and above board. I have attached my CV for your perusal, and I look forward to hearing from you soon.

Kind regards

Ian Carpenter

OK, what's next? St George's – deadline: 19/10/07. Mentoring and Befriending – deadline: 8/10/07. Southend College – deadline: 12/10/07 (pants, that one was local too!). West Midlands Police – deadline: 15/10/07. Amnesty International – deadline: 15/10/07 (not that I'd have applied anyway). Arts Educational School – deadline: 8/10/07. I think spot a trend here. Hello? A reply from the London Business School already –

Thank you,

your application/query has been received. We
will be in touch with you in due course,

Regards

Recruitment Administrator

This is an automated email, please do not
respond

OK, I won't. And thanks. Here's a little update for anyone
concerned about Lenny's ear: it does appear to be healing,
and it does not smell so much now. There were a few days
there when we did not sit next to each other on the bus.
I was on one side of the aisle, and he was sat on the other.
Well, I didn't want him catching my stomach bug.

Friday 2nd November 2007

I returned to work today to 60 odd emails. That'll teach me for being sick. Gearing up to sort through all the madness that had gone on in my absence, I opened this from my boss, Steve:

To: Ian Carpenter

Subject: A bad day for france

Nobby 2 v 6 Eddie

1st leg southend to brentford

Eddie raced into an almost immediate lead on joining M25 but could not hold on as I entered Hertfordshire. 1 - 1. South Mimms appears to be temporarily French?? 2 - 1. Imagine my delight when Eddie rammed home a hattrick in the space of a minute! 2 - 4. I must admit to a small shout of 'yes'. Is that wrong? Despite 3 James Irlam pitch invasions Eddie kept the pressure on and the fifth was slotted in just after the M1. 2 - 5. A cheeky sixth at Rickmansworth finished off the Frenchies. 2 - 6. Bring on the 2nd leg. Report to follow.

And, indeed, a report did follow:

To: Ian Carpenter

Subject: Putting England back on the map

Nobby 4 v 7 Eddie

6 - 13 On aggregate

2nd leg brentford to southend

After a wasted journey to Brentford I was looking forward to the 2nd leg with a very comfortable margin. Started well. Two early Eddie's just after M4 and just before M1. 0 - 2. Needing a pee I turned off a South Mimms. On the slip road I pulled up behind a Nobby. The ref would not listen to my cries of offside. 1 - 2. Possibly enjoying this too much?? A turn for the worse when Nobby brought out the big guns - 2 tankers at the Holmesdale tunnel. 3 - 2. I suspect the dirty burger van man was making a killing in Waltham Abbey - another hattrick for Eddie! 3 - 5. A straggler just after that made it 3 - 6. The A12 gave Nobby a consolation. 4 - 6. I thought that would be that until just as I was turning off at the A127 Eddie started to run round the Frenchies with his willy hanging out. 4 - 7. What a fantastic game of Norbert Dentressangle V Eddie Stobart! 6-13 on aggregate!

I can see this game catching on. Not only that, but it put my game on the way to Feltham into absolute shame. Good work, Steve. Anyway, tonight I got in and there was no food in the house. Not surprising, as I'd been cooped up in bed for a couple of days and Nicky's been working very hard of late. I decided to test the Doctor's potion by having an Indian meal delivered. Kill or cure, I reckon. For the record: chicken rogan josh, pilau rice, naan, vegetable passanda, and some onion bahjees.

I had no responses from potential employers today but I do have some big news: the smoking spider went on a little adventure this evening. She normally never ventures beyond the picture rail but tonight she was a window's-length away from home! Perhaps she was inspired by our epic journey to Switzerland last weekend. The picture shows our unusual arachnid enjoying the joys of nicotine – she's just a little to the right of the glove:

I've never seen a health warning on the side of a cigarette packet that says smoking is harmful to spiders around you, so I think I'm on safe ground when it comes to the RSPCA and such like. Hold on, is that a couple more orbs... ?

Sunday 4th November 2007

We went to a housewarming-come-bonfire party last night. That kind of works; 'let's warm the house by lighting a great big fire!'. I don't know why more people don't wait until Bonfire Night to finalise their house purchases. I reckon one of the guests must have been in the Boy Scouts when they were younger. When the fireworks started, he not only pulled out a paparazzi-grade camera, but he also erected a tripod! Is it just me, or is that a little *too* prepared? –

Tripod Camera Man: Hello Marge [partner of Tripod Camera Man], don't forget we're going to that party tonight, so we need to get a few things to bring.

Marge: Oh yes, I'll get some flowers for the hosts, a bottle of red and a bottle of white wine.

Tripod Camera Man: I'll get a card from the shop, oh, and I'll also pack that really professional looking camera tripod in order to take pictures of the fireworks.

I also played a short game of Mornington Crescent with Simon by text:

Me: Fancy a game of Mornington Crescent? Normal Rules, bi-laterals count double. I'll start by sacrificing Seven Sisters: Tooting Bec.

Simon: I'm afraid that makes no sense to me. You should apply anyway.

Me: Sorry, it's from *I'm Sorry I haven't a Clue*. It's game where there are no rules. You make your own rules up. Your turn.

Simon: I take Pimlico and raise you a Cockfosters.

Me: Ah, you've been studying the Karpov Dilemma. Forward counts for three, and I have a Community Chest. So: Friern Barnet.

Simon: Predictable. Friern Barnet is a type 2 so I have to employ the Yuri Gargarin method. Over the river puts me in a bit of a fix, but I'm afraid it's Whitechapel.

Me: Mornington Crescent (denotes end of game).

Simon's first game of Mornington Crescent – jammy bugger, isn't he? Short game though, they can go on for months. Anyone who wants to see how the pro's do it should visit the Radio Four message board on bbc.co.uk. On a more sobering note, I'm now looking at my jobs page and I have to admit I'm becoming a bit disheartened. Most of the jobs on page ten have passed their apply-by date. I need to move faster from now on.

Monday 5th November 2007

The Zygos Partnership have finally turned me down:

RESEARCH CONSULTANT POSITION

Thank you for your email enclosing a copy of your CV with reference to the above role which I have read with care. There have been a number of candidates who more closely match the skills set and experience required for this position, so unfortunately on this occasion, you have not been successful in your application. Nevertheless, may I take this opportunity to thank you for writing to The Zygos Partnership and wish you every success with your future career.

Yours sincerely

The Zygos Partnership

Oh well, at least I won't be found hanging from Neap Bridge. As discussed above – well I say 'discussed', more like 'mentioned' – the jobs on this page are no more, they have expired, they have ceased to be. Dear reader, please feel free to let your mind wander as I mention all the expired jobs and their apply-by dates: *[list cut, because it is unwise to encourage readers to allow their minds to wander. Ed.]* One little gem at the end has no reply by date: English

Language Sales Manager for Ivy Group. Apparently I have to apply to someone called Alistair Campbell. It can't be. Surely not? –

Dear Alistair

I note with some considerable interest your position for English Language Sales Manager advertised in The Guardian dated 29/09/07. Firstly, are you really Alistair Campbell? If so, I have bought your book, The Tony Blair Years. I have to admit that I have been a bit busy recently, so I have not had a chance to read it from cover to cover. However, whenever I get a spare couple of weeks, I will give it my full attention. I am not sure exactly what the advertisement meant. Do I have to sell the English language to other people? I would welcome some clarification on this matter. I have attached my CV for your perusal, and I look forward to hearing from you soon.

Kind regards

Ian Carpenter

Page ten done!

Tuesday 6th November 2007

Stop with the fireworks already, please! Lenny and Hippy
are totally freaked out. OK, page 11 and, sadly, a bunch
of them are past the use-by date too, so I won't mention
those. However, Tuffin Ferraby Taylor are still 'looking for
an individual to define strategy and manage delivery of all
central global marketing activity and communications.' –

Dear Madam/Sir

I am writing regarding your advertisement in
the Guardian dated 29/09/07. Your advertisement
asked that I define strategy. Well, according to
my Griffin Savers Oxford Dictionary (1984):

'1. the planning and direction of the whole
operation of a campaign or war.

2. a plan policy of this kind or to achieve
something, our economic strategy.'

I hope that I have successfully defined strategy, and
I do hope that you are not asking people to direct
a war. I have attached my CV for your perusal, and
I look forward to hearing from you soon.

Kind regards

Ian Carpenter

Other developments: Lenny's ear now smells only mildly unpleasant and our spider seems to be cutting down on her smoking.

Thursday 8th November 2007

GREETINGS!

From Mrs Maria Elena Fernandez,

I am the above named person from Philippine. I am married to Mr. Rodolfo FERNANDEZ who worked with Philippine embassy in Kuwait for nine years before we left to Philippine where he was re-appointed as a navy officer before his untimely death in the year 2005. We were married for eleven years without a child. He died in his home country Philippine after a brief illness that lasted for only four days Before his death we were both born again Christian. Since his death I decided not to remarry or get a child outside my matrimonial home which the Bible is against. When my late husband was alive he deposited the sum of $7.3Musd (Seven Million Three Hundred Thousand U.S. Dollars) in cash concealed in a trunk box and deposits it with a Security Company in Abidjan Cote d ivoire (West Africa) which he declare and register it as family valuables. Recently, my Doctor told me that i have serious sickness which is cancer problem. The one that disturbs me most is the high blood pressure sickness. Having known my condition I decided to donate this fund to a church or individual that will utilize this money the way I am going to instruct herein. I want a church or individual that will use this fund for orphanages, widows, propagating the word of God and to endeavour that the house of God is maintained. The Bible made us to understand that Blessed is the hand that giveth I took this decision because I do not have any child that will inherit this money and my husband relatives are not Christians and I do not want my husband's efforts to be used by unbelievers. This is why I am taking this decision to contact you. I am not afraid of death hence I know where I am going. I know that I am going to be in the bosom of the Lord. Exodus 14 VS 14 says that the lord will fight my case and I shall hold my peace. I do not need any telephone communication for security purpose until this mission is accomplished. With God all things are possible. As soon as I receive your reply with full assurance of your assistance, I shall give you the legal proof of this matter and contact of the security company in Abidjan where he deposited the trunk box. I will also issue you an authority letter that will prove you the present and legal beneficiary of this trunk box (fund). I want you and the church to always pray for me because the lord is my shepherd. My happiness is that I lived a life of a worthy Christian. Whoever that wants to serve the Lord must serve him in Spirit and Truth.

Hope to receive your reply.

Remain blessed in the Lord.

Yours in Christ,

Mrs Maria Elena Fernandez

Hmm... It looks like the good people from the Complementry (their spelling) Art Gallery have not wasted time in sharing my personal details. Well, stable doors and horses and all that, better just get on with the job –

Dear Joanna

I read with delight your advertisement for a subscriptions manager in The Guardian dated 29/09/07. I apologise in the lateness of my reply. You say in your advert that languages are useful, but not essential. As you can see from my attached CV, I can speak several languages. I would like to consider myself a polyglot! However, what I find most interesting, is working with my own language. For instance, in work the other day, someone bought some strawberry iced fingers. Inside the strawberry fingers was a layer of strawberry jam. I was concerned that this might be a bit too much strawberry for one snack. I therefore asked the question if this was a little too strawberry-y (like sugary or salty). Try it,

it is a great word: Strawberry-y! Should you have
any queries about my CV, please do not hesitate
to contact me.

Kind regards

Ian Carpenter

End of page 11! And page twelve looks great – only eight
jobs. OK, one from 'COI' – what does that stand for? Am I
going to be working for Japanese fish? They wanted a live
event co-ordinator, and an event assistant, but unfortunately
the apply-by date was 8/10/07. Interviews for Haringey
Council will be held 'towards the end of October'. Well
you can never plan these things at a local council. I mean,
how much time does it take to order the correct biscuits
for the Annual General Meeting? This reminds me, I still
haven't followed the Liberal Democrats leadership process
through. I'll do this once I've applied for this next one:

**Jolly Learning has leadership internationally in synthetic
phonics publishing. Indeed, in several countries, the
majority of countries teach reading with our programme
(including the UK).**

Oh, they want me to write. I'm out of stationery. It'll have
to wait.

Saturday 10th November 2007

Today we went to the supermarket. Why do posh people in four-by-fours get to park near the entrance? Oh yes, they have children. Don't get me started on 4 x 4s. When we got home, I was delighted that the indoor bowls was on the telly, live from the International Hall, Ponds Forge, Sheffield. Paul Foster v David Gourlay; what a game! Paul Foster has hair like Tintin. It came down to a tie-break. David Gourlay went for a runner when he should have gone for a draw shot, apparently. 1-0 Foster. With a tricky jack-length of 28m, Gourlay drew even, but Foster eventually won 4-8,11-3,2-1. The other semi-final was between Alex Marshall MBE (MBE? For services to bowls?) and Jason Greenslade. Greenslade won, so we can look forward to a thrilling final tomorrow.

Sunday 11th November 2007

I was listening to the food programme on Radio Four this afternoon. They were talking about how the future reduction in EU sugar quotas was going to have a detrimental effect on the economies of the Caribbean. It reminded me of that old joke:

Person A: I'm taking my wife to the Caribbean.

Person B: Jamaica?

Person A: No, she wanted to go.

I wonder if it works with other Caribbean islands –

A: I am taking my wife, Anna, to the Caribbean

B: Guiana?

A: No, she's a woman.

Hmmm, maybe not. Down to business: the Food Standards Agency are looking for a Senior Press Officer. Apparently, 'Food has never been a bigger concern of the British public'. Let's be honest about this, ever since the cavemen days, food has been a fairly high concern with the general populace. Encams want a Market Research Manager. Thankfully, this is a charity that deals with food and stuff. I say 'thankfully', because it means I can't apply for it – the job was based in Wigan; what a commute that would have been. And I can't apply to agencies, as it would be never ending... look, here's one: The Works: 'Weary of your host? Use our Search Engine.' Well, I have been reading the same jobs paper for about a month and a half now, so I am a bit weary of it. Let's have a look at what they've got —

Select type:
Any

Select Sector:
Any

Select level:
Any

Select Location:
Any

Click...

229 Jobs!!! See? That would be ridiculous.

Monday 12th November 2007

Yesterday's highly anticipated bowls final was superb. It went right down to a tie break but Paul 'Fozzy' Foster won through in the end. Why do they spray a bowl that's touched the jack with breath freshener? I don't know. Not only did I watch the bowls yesterday, but I also bought a book on origami. This photo shows my first effort at creating 'Saturn' – I hope you like it:

Well, on we go: Guardian Media Group wants an auditor. They should audit their job adverts more frequently as some of them are distinctly dodgy. Entry date for that one passed some time ago, unfortunately. Dow Jones Newswires in Frankfurt want some people for 7 different jobs. No problem, seven birds with one stone –

Dear all

I would like to apply for your jobs in the Guardian
dated 29/09/07. Please find attached my CV for
your perusal.

Kind regards

Ian Carpenter

Financial Times are looking for a Chief Sub-Editor, a
Sub-Editor, a Deputy Production Editor, and a further
Sub Editor. OK –

Dear Madam/Sir

I note that you have several positions advertised
in the Guardian dated 29/09/07. I do apologise
for the lateness in my reply, but I have been
applying for quite a number of jobs recently. As
you can see from my attached CV, I worked in a
bank for ten years. How financial is that? I look
forward to hearing from you soon.

Yours sincerely

Ian Carpenter

Tuesday 13th November 2007

They discovered another case of bird flu today. H5N1, apparently. What kind of a name is that for a disease? Ridiculous. Hmmm, I should imagine that if you were a bird, and you had flu, it would be quite hard to fly without banging into trees or lampposts. I mean, it's hard enough to type whilst sneezing, let alone fly. You might even end up flying upside down. That reminds me; I was once told by one of my lecturers at university that if you want to see how unequal the world is, get a map of the world and turn it upside down. Good advice I reckon. Just thought I'd share that. Anyway, here's one for Foxtons, they're opening a new branch for Dulwich and Woking. Foxtons. We've all seen them driving about in those Mini Coopers. I really do not want to work for these people but given my background in the mortgage and property business, it seems inevitable that they'd want to interview me. I'll have to try really hard not to get this one. No email option. I have to call them. It's 10 p.m. I don't think even the hard working go-getters will be there now. I'll have to call them during the day. They have a picture of someone kite-surfing in their advert. Do they do a lot of kite-surfing in Woking? Onwards: the Overseas Development Institute wants a Head of Communications – charity; VPS Consultancy – see above; Media PA, hello – 'ideal candidate will have varied media experience, be highly organised and used to working to deadlines. An ability to speak French is desirable'. Perfect –

Dear Alan

I read with incredulity your advertisement for a job in the Guardian dated 29/09/07. I am honest, trustworthy and discreet. My mother once bought a Cindy doll for my sister for Christmas, which I found in the cupboard at the start of December. I did not let on once to my sister! I can also speak French. Please find attached my CV for your perusal, and I look forward to hearing from you soon.

Kind regards

Ian Carpenter

End of page 13 – woo!

Wednesday 14th November 2007

Dear Ian

On behalf of the Board of the International Institute of Communications may I thank you for kindly submitting details of your experience for the post of Director General at the Institute. We had a number of applicants and it was very hard to get to a reasonable short list. We have chosen three whose experience pattern is very close to what we require so I regret that we will not be able to take your own application forward at this time. We do wish you success in your search for a suitable post.

Best regards,

Sebastian Mann
Projects Executive
International Institute of Communications

I applied for this job on the 3rd October. They *are* the Institute of Communications so they must have had to talk about it for a while, but six weeks must be considered procrastination. I've just been checking flights to Frankfurt for the Job at Dow Jones. I feel I have to go. It would be wrong of me to warrant Patrick Meiier of ACM Markets a visit in Geneva and not visit Dow Jones. I wonder how leathery the sofa is in the foyer of *their* building? I could go this weekend; I have a day off on Friday. I asked Nicky, but she didn't seem interested so I might have to go on my own. Maybe I should wait until Johann has considered my application. OK, what's next: UCL want a Manager of the Multimedia Unit – apply by date was 5/10/07. The Shoreditch Trust wants a Marketing, Arts and Events Assistant – interview date was 22/10/07, and it's a charity. However, I was in Shoreditch only last week at a property that I manage. I like the area, and Nicky's an art teacher... No, it is a charity, move on: The Courtauld Institute of Art want an Education Programmes Co-ordinator – interview date: 19/10/07. The British Red Cross want several Campaigns people: 'c.24K incl. ILW dependent on experience'. I see. Language evolves. Too late for that one also. University of London want a Head of Internal Communications and External Relations, and Lime Pictures wanted a Broadcast Engineer to work on Hollyoaks. Ditto x2. What's a 'Stakeholder Engagement Officer'? Tower Hamlets council wanted three of them but they all had to apply by 12/10/07. This page is not looking very good on the application front. Not a single job applied for. But Breakthrough Breast Cancer has brightened up my day with their purple advert – please feel free to donate money to these people. Page 14 done!

Animal News Update: the smoking spider has given up the ghost for the winter; it's too cold. And Lenny's ear has

more or less completely healed. I wonder when the fur
will grow back on it, though. He does look a bit odd with
one bald ear.

Thursday 15th November 2007

I'm taking a break from the project this evening. I've just been watching Nick Clegg and Chris Huhne arguing the same point with each other on Question Time. The Lib Dems missed a trick by not appointing me as their leader. Them and the International Institute of Communications. When will they learn? Anyway, here's a picture of Lenny sitting on the bus:

You may notice a little 'v' in his left ear. It's an old battle wound. We sometimes call him Len-v.

Friday 16th November 2007

I was doing some research for the Liberal Democrat Project. I noticed the following on their site:

Vince Cable

Following the resignation of Ming Campbell as party leader, his deputy Dr Vincent Cable has become Acting Leader pending a leadership election. You can read about Vince Cable on his biography page.

What do you think of that? Should you not spell it Menzies? Perhaps they've been hanging out with the good people at The Jolly Learning Partnership. Remember them from Thursday 8th November? They're the ones peddling phonics. If I ever get to become an MP for the Liberal Democrats, maybe I'll be known as Eeyanne. OK, Islington Borough Council are loooking for a Corporate Communications Officer, Communications and Marketing Officers (x2), and a Senior Media Officer. Apply by date was 14th October 2007. I reflected for a moment on the sad irony of their written suggestion to call them 'if you require this document in large print or braille'. Flight Centre want Sales Consultants who have visited two continents outside europe. Hmm, I haven't done this. Never mind; I never much fancied Sales Consultancy. The next job Assistant Editor for the

UK Independent Party! My political leanings are being pushed from pillar to post here. As luck would have it, the apply by date was 3/10/07. Blimey, you had to be quick with that lot. Next it's AS & K Mercury Healthcare Communications, 'a leading communications agency providing innovative and strategically focussed solutions across the pharmaceutical industry'. They're looking for an Editor and an Assistant Editor. Great –

Dear Madam/Sir

I have come across your advertisement for the above positions in the Guardian dated 29/09/07. I do not have a biomedical degree or a life science degree. I did however get an A in GCSE biology. I am interested in medical issues and Healthcare communications. I particularly like the anti-smoking poster where the cigarette turns into a tube of fatty cholesterol. I have attached my CV for your perusal, and I look forward to your reply.

Kind regards

Ian Carpenter

TESCO would 'like to get closer to the communities we serve'. Really? There's already one large TESCO and four baby TESCOs within walking distance of my house, now they're looking to put an even bigger TESCO about 800 yards nearer my house than the existing big one. How many toasters for £2.97 can they sell? The person that you had to apply to, by the 5th October, was David Younghusband. Sorry Marike, you've just moved into second place in the top five list of peculiar names I've encountered on my little quest. The list now looks like this:

1. David Younghusband
2. Marike Dippenaar
3. Sir Menzies Campbell (phonetically Ming)
4. Orkan Ahmadov
5. Patrick Meiier

One more: Ofcom wants a Partner. That's a bit forward for a first encounter, but OK... Ah – apply by 8/10/07. Probably for the best.

Saturday 17th November 2007

United Nations Secretary, Ban Ki-moon, has called for action on climate change at next month's Climate Change conference in Bali. He was introducing the Intergovernmental Panel on Climate Change report. I really hope there's a job with the United Nations in the next 14 pages of my Guardian Work section, not because I care passionately about the environment, but because Ban Ki-moon would easily make the top five peculiar names list. Email from the Financial Times:

Thank you for your application. If you do not hear from us in the next 4 weeks your application has been unsuccessful at this time. However, your information will be stored electronically for six months in case any other suitable vacancies become available, with access limited to managers responsible for recruitment. If you don't wish us to keep your details on file please notify us by return.

They plan to keep my details on file for six months? I was hoping this would all be over, well, certainly by January. This could drag it out until May next year. That's 180 more days! Anyway, on with the jobs... Rambert Dance Company wanted a Head of Revenue Fund Raising. ABD (Apply By Date): 11/10/07. I am quite relieved by this; my partner used to work for a dance company and

I've seen some very odd, if not disturbing contemporary dance in my time. Next it's Wiley 1807–2007 Knowledge for Generations. They've been around for two hundred years and, to be perfectly honest, I'd never heard of them. What do they do?

We currently have an opportunity for a Market Development Manager to join our Market Development department.

That make sense, you wouldn't want them in the frozen food department.

A good Knowledge of Wiley-Blackwell products, sales channels, and business models is desirable.

Blackwell do books I think. Lets have a look at their website... OK, Wiley has now bought up Blackwell Books:

In 1807, Charles Wiley, then 25 years old, opened a small printing shop at 6 Reade Street in lower Manhattan, New York City. During the next four years, he worked with other printers, primarily Isaac Riley, printing and publishing law books. In 1812, "C. Wiley, Printer" appeared for the first time on the title pages of several legal works. Two years later, Charles Wiley formed a printing, publishing, and bookselling partnership with Cornelius Van Winkle, a noted printer, located at 3 Wall Street. At this site Wiley also hosted the "Den," a meeting place for writers such

as James Fenimore Cooper and William Cullen Bryant that foreshadowed the Greenwich Village coffee houses of the 1950s. Wiley and Van Winkle ended their partnership in 1820, when Charles chose to focus on publishing and bookselling and began hiring others to do his printing. He published James Fenimore Cooper's *The Spy* in 1821 and helped to launch this first American novelist's career. Wiley also published works by Richard Henry Dana, Washington Irving, and many other writers.

Cornelius Van Winkle would definitely make the peculiar names list. Sadly, the apply by date has passed (15/10/07) but, happily, I've reached the end of page 15 and passed the half way mark!!! Page 16 looks a lot more of a colourful affair than some of the other pages. We have pink, peach, and blue adverts on this page. The Arch Nemesis is looking for a Head of Marketing and Communications. I think their communications are quite good. They've declined me on a Sunday Morning in a mere five minutes before now. Hmmm... 'Positive about mental health'... 'This trust operates a smoke-free policy'... The apply by date's been and gone, I'm not sorry to report. Encams are looking for a Media and Communications Manager. I have come across these people before (see Sunday 11/11/07), they were looking for a Market Research Manager. They could have saved a few quid by putting them together in one advert. Anyway, I am still relieved that they're a charity; I really wouldn't want to commute to Wigan. The Guardian is looking for a 'Commercialbrandmanager' – come on, that's a ridiculous typo. They also got about half the page... Well it is their newspaper I suppose, and it's in peach. 'The CBM will be expected to employ a variety of ATL.' I hope that's clear. Apply by date was 15/10/07. Brand Recruitment are looking for a Senior PR Executive and a Head of PR/Brand Experience FMCG/Leisure. No apply by date! Here goes –

Dear Madam/Sir

I have happened upon your advertisement in the Guardian dated 29/10/07. Your advertisement asked that I have a strong PR background preferably from financial services. I clearly do not have any PR experience, but I did work in a bank for ten years. My only concern about your advertisement is that you mention: 'This role will involve formulating strategic direction for the PR function and liaising with press at a high level as well as occasionally 'digging in' at events!!' Whilst I have no objection to formulating the strategic direction (as long as you aren't planning to start a war), I am unable to dig in, as I have a bad back. Will this affect my chances of employment in any way? I have attached my CV for your perusal, and I look forward to hearing from you soon.

Kind regards

Ian Carpenter

Sunday 18th November 2007

I received a fantastic email this afternoon. Can you guess who it was from? It was from Nicky's Mum, Jean. It turns out she has been reading the blog, and was taken with the origami:

```
Hi Eeeeeeyan

Just thought you would like a look at the following
site:
```

www.britishorigami.info

```
Who would have thought it? Methinks they are
Liberals - the beards are the giveaway !!!!!!! As
an origami man have you heard of Thoki Yen?

Sadly now deceased.

Love

Jean
```

Brilliant! OK, on with the jobs. 'Smg is seeking 4 sales executives to join our dynamic team in Amsterdam.' Great, as discussed above, I lived in Holland for a brief period. It would be nice to go back and meet up with Jaques and the others. No apply by date so here we go –

Dear Tracey Van Gessel

I read with wonder your advertisement for Sales executives to join your team in Amsterdam. Your advertisement stated that I should visit your website, which I have done. It also requested that I send a motivating letter, so here is my attempt: A week ago, I did not know how to do origami, but I bought a book. I have attached a picture of a 'Space Ship' that I created this afternoon. You see, anything is possible!!! I hope that this is motivating enough, and I have attached my CV for your perusal.

Kind regards

Ian Carpenter

And look at this one:

THE CITY COUNCIL OF LIVERPOOL PROCUREMENT SUPPORT UNIT CONTRACT 1089

Why all capitals? As discussed above, I'm a keen supporter of Liverpool Football Club – if you remember, it cost me the Manager's job at Tottenham Hotspur – so I am most intrigued by this job.

The questionaire document can be downloaded from the Liverpool City Council website at www.liverpool. gov.uk Go to A-Z of service, p for procurement unit, then current tenders

'Procurement unit'? Lets have a little look at the site:

<u>**Advert Q10182 Safeguarding Adults – Investigative Skills**</u>

<u>**Quote Q10182 Safeguarding Adults – Investigative Skills**</u>

<u>**Advert Q10187 HUB 2008 – Temporary Skate Park**</u>

<u>**Quote Q10187 HUB 2008 – Temporary Skate Park**</u>

<u>**Advert Q10189 Liverpool Capital of Culture Events 2008 - Economic Impact Assessment**</u>

<u>**Quote Q10189 Liverpool Capital of Culture Events 2008 -**</u>

Economic Impact Assessment

Advert STQ060 Kitchen Equipment for Catering Services

Quote STQ060 Kitchen Equipment for Catering Services

Advert STQ061 Home Improvement Packs (HIPS)

Quote STQ061 Home Improvement Packs (HIPS)

Advert STQ062 Hire of Pianos and Equipment

Quote STQ062 Hire of Pianos and Equipment

Advert STQ063 Production of a Short Video

Quote STQ063 Production of a Short Video

As you can see, there's a lot going on in Liverpool at the moment. I couldn't possibly apply for all of these tenders, that would be ridiculous, however, the Hire of Pianos and Equipment does interest me:

INVITATION TO QUOTE
STQ 062
Hire of Pianos /Equipment plus Piano Tuner

Liverpool City Council on behalf of the Liverpool Culture Company is looking to appoint a supplier to provide the hire of 4 Pianos plus a piano tuner and other related equipment. Please see quotation document for specification requirements. For further information or to arrange a site visit please contact [name deleted]. The quotation document may be downloaded from the Liverpool City Council website at www.liverpool.gov.uk Go to A-Z of council services, for procurement unit, then current tenders. Closing date for receipt of completed quotations is 10.00am Friday, 14th December 2007.

I read the tender request. It was sublime. About 100 pages of clauses in order to hire four pianos plus a piano tuner. It must have taken them the best part of a year to draw it all up. Endless meetings. And what about ordering the Rich Teas? Do they have to put that job out to tender? It would probably look a bit like this:

INVITATION TO QUOTE
STQ 063
Supply of Rich Tea Biscuits/Digestives plus biscuit taster

Liverpool City Council on behalf of the Liverpool Culture Company is looking to appoint a supplier to provide the supply of 4 packets of biscuits plus a biscuit taster and other related equipment. Please see quotation document for specification requirements. For further information or to arrange a site visit please contact [name deleted]. The quotation document may be downloaded from the Liverpool City Council website at www.liverpool.gov.uk Go to A-Z of council services, for procurement unit, then current tenders.

Closing date for receipt of completed applications is 11.00am Friday, as that is when we are meeting to discuss the proposal for changing from PG Tips to Tetley (subject to approval by the Council).

Monday 19th November 2007

Today I got another email from my boss:

Thurs 15 Nov
Floodlit game Leamington Spa to Basildon
Nobby 9 v 8 Stobby

Dear Ian

Didn't play the trip to Leamington thankfully, too many Frenchies about.

Was heading for a disaster game as the M40 left Stobby trailing 5 - 1!! Zut Alors! On the M25 I saw a lorry emblazoned Carpenters. Just thought you might like to know. Unusually saw 2 Tate and Lyle tankers - but they could not be counted. You have to have rules. Without rules where would we be? France. M25 was kind - in terms of the game, not the damn traffic. After thinking the thrashing on the M40 was irreversable the score was hauled back to 6 all! Just after the A10 our hearts were broken by the sight of a Nobby 7 - 6. Bugger. A Nobby tanker rubbed salt in the wound at the A12 before another Stobby restored hope 8 - 7. Unbelievably a Nobby was ambling along in the queue for the A127 9 - 7. Despite a late Stobby just by the turn off it ended 9 - 8. Merde.

Steve

Good game. Al Murray, the pub landlord, would be happy
with the anti-French stuff. Yes, it is a parody ladies and
gentlemen. Anyway, I got loads of emails today:

Dear Ian

Thank you for your recent application via Marketing
Jobboard. Unfortunately your skills and experience
do not match what we are looking for at this time.
However, we will keep your details on file and if
your skills and experience match a specific role,
we will be the first to contact you! If you wish
to be removed from our records, please email us
at info@brandrecruitment.co.uk .

We wish you all the best in your future career.

All best,

Jayde

I think it was the comment about my bad back, and not
wanting to dig in. And there was this:

Dear Ian,

Thank you for your CV and covering letter.   We

have no immediate positions, however, we will keep
your details on file for 6 months and we will be
in contact should a suitable opportunity arise.
If you do not wish us to keep your details on
file please notify us by return.

Best Wishes

Caroline Garside
HR Administrator

What? You were the ones that advertised in The Guardian,
I know you have positions! –

Dear Caroline

Thank you for your email. I have to admit that I was
a bit surprised, as I was applying for positions
that you have advertised. However, I am pleased
that you are keeping my details on file, and I look
forward to hearing from you in the near future.

Kind regards

Ian Carpenter

Anyway, I got into work early this morning. I had a chat
with Melissa and Laura from our accounts department
and brought my interest in the fine art of origami to their
attention. Within ten minutes I had a crane mum and
baby on my desk. They are fantastic!

Tuesday 20th November 2007

Today I received an extensive Guardianjobs enewsletter. They're really taking the proverbial now. Still, I suppose it's not too serious when you consider today's news that the Government have given away the personal details of 25 million people. This includes bank details, names and addresses of everyone in the UK that qualifies for family tax credits. Certainly puts my little problem with the Complementry Art Gallery into perspective. On a lighter note, Simon and I have tried to organise the inaugural meeting of the Southend Poppadom Society in an Indian restaurant on Friday night. I'm trying to get some takers, but nobody seems interested. Let's see what happens. And some Animal News: the smoking spider has really ceased to be. Hippy and Lenny are OK, and greatly relieved that the fireworks have dissipated. OK, on with the jobs... Oh no wait. Paranormal Barry has been doing some repairs on a property I manage. He sent me a picture of some fences that he's been working on. Guess what? Another orb: *[but not a particularly good one, and not worth reproducing here. Ed.].* OK: Senior Public Affairs Manager at energywatch – ABD: 15/10/07. Casual Subeditors for Observer Sport. I suppose I wouldn't have to wear a tie – ABD: 7/10/07. End of page 16, and page 17 looks a bit posh – I think I'll leave it until tomorrow. I've also been trying to purloin pianos from various people at work. They all seem to have friends who own them, but are unwilling to lend them to me for use by The City Council of Liverpool.

Wednesday 21st October 2007

No emails received today. Perhaps everyone was down the pub watching England get beaten 3-2 by Croatia. I thought it was a fairly exciting game, despite everyone's doom and gloom. So on with posh page 17:

Jane's Information Group offers a range of integrated advertising, intelligence and consultancy solutions in five specialist areas – defence, security, transport, public safety and law enforcement.

Hmm, 'enforcement' again. Better tread carefully –

Dear Emma

I read with interest your advertisements in the Guardian dated 29/09/07. I appreciate that I am slightly late in responding, but I would still like to apply. Firstly, I can't help mentioning that you have missed a trick. You are marketing your organisation as Jane's. Jane's Information Group would lend itself to the acronym JIG. Just think of the possibilities!!! JIGSAW – a monthly newsletter, where you tell everyone about the defence, security, transport, public safety and law enforcement that you have observed over the last month. Let's JIG! A once a month party when all like-minded people can have a bit of a boogie, whilst discussing defence, security, etc. I hope you are interested in my ideas. I have attached my CV for your perusal and I look forward to hearing from you soon.

Kind regards

Ian Carpenter

Sheridan Edward at Modern Art Oxford – charity. Titan Publishing Group want editors for comics, and designers. Apply by 28/09/07. What?!? The paper was published on the 29/09/07! –

Dear Madam/Sir

I was stupefied by your advert in the Guardian dated 29/09/07. Your advert asked that I apply for the job by the 28/09/07. Are you really expecting people to have developed a time machine? I appreciate that you are publishing comics, but in the real world, I do not think that is possible. However, I would like to try. An associate of mine, who I call Paranormal Barry, could probably assist. Whenever he takes a photo, funny orbs appear in it. I have attached my CV for your perusal, and I look forward to your earliest reply.

Kind regards

Ian Carpenter

Two small adverts in the corner ask no more from applicants than a CV –

```
Dear Madam/Sir

Please find attached my CV.

Kind regards

Ian Carpenter
```

Can you imagine next summer, when the European championships are on? No UK teams. Oh well, at least the gutters will not be full of those stupid flags that have fallen off the car windows. Every cloud...

Thursday 22nd November 2007

I was mortally embarrassed today. I went to the supermarket after work and I was forced to go to the check-out of the woman that saw me topless on the stage of the Southend Cliffs Pavilion, serenading Julian Clary whilst having my nipples rubbed by his erstwhile sidekick, Hugh Jelly (from sticky moments). I managed to avoid her for about four years since the incident, but she was right on the end of the line of checkouts. I went bright red. I should just explain that I went to see Julian Clary about four years ago. I was selected to participate in his live show. I say selected, the bloke in front of me refused to go up and it really forced my hand. Anyway, after I'd answered several questions about my favourite sexual positions etc., the 600 odd people in the audience were greatly amused to learn that I worked in a bank. The following day, Nicky and I went to the supermarket, and the check out person said "Were you at the Cliffs Pavilion last night?" I could have died. She still remembers the incident, apparently, even after four years. I still have the bottle of champagne that I was given that night and, yes, I do have a picture. So on with the admin'. Jane's Information Group has sent me an email:

Dear Ian,

Sorry could you just clarify which position you

would like to apply for.

Many thanks,

Emma Cussel
Resource and Development Administrator

No probs, Emma –

Dear Emma

Thank you for your email. Please, do not apologise for asking for clarification of my application. I have to admit, it was not clear from my original email. I would like to apply for both positions advertised. They were, in turn: Deputy Editor, Jane's Defence Weekly-Coulsdon Surrey, and, Chief Sub-Editor (Defence and Transport)-Coulsdon Surrey. I hope that this clarifies the matter, and I look forward to hearing from you soon.

Kind regards

Ian Carpenter

I also received this odd email:

Dear Ian

Regards

Craig Cobb
Consultant
Judd Farris Property Recruitment

Hmmm –

Dear Craig

Thank you for your email. I noted with a considerable amount of interest that you did not include a message. The more you know, the less you need to show, I suppose.

Kind regards

Ian Carpenter

Admin' over.

Friday 23rd November 2007

I have the day off today, so I naturally have time on my hands. And there is no better way to kill time than by playing Googlewhack. This was inspired by a book by Dave Gorman called The Goolgewhack Adventure. The idea is that you put two random words into Google to see if you get only one hit. Guess what? 'guardianwork rogan' is a Googlewhack!! Fantastic! The internet is a marvellous thing. I've been on Blogspot only a few weeks, but if you put just 'guardianwork' into google, there are twenty hits and my blog comes up first. And I haven't paid Google a penny! And 'guardianwork' is in there with the links to 'A love of food, food for love – romantic recipes' and (because of my very first job application with the NHS) 'http://www.isthisyour.name/joe_gibson.htm'. Incredible! OK, down to business, and this one's a big one – yesterday at work it was pointed out to me, by Laura, Dan, Barry and Martin, that there is a new vacant position. The England boss, Steve McLaren, has lost his job following Wednesday night's defeat. I reckon it's time for bonus job number 3! I'll have a look at the vacancies section of the FA site:

The Football Association is committed to our vision of using the power of football to build a better future.

The core objectives that support the achievement of

this are:

- To be seen by fans, players, managers, clubs and the government as the leading sports governing body in the world
- To lead the development of a grass-roots framework which will achieve the highest levels of participation in the world
- To achieve consistent, long-term success on the field through player development at every level
- To be a leading-edge marketing organisation
- To lead and shape the debate about football at a national, UEFA and FIFA level
- To provide leading-edge service levels both internally and externally

If this sounds like the type of organisation that you would like to be part of, then see and revisit this section for information on Vacancies.

FA Vacancies

There are no other vacancies at present

What are they talking about!? The whole world knows McLaren's been sacked!

Sunday 25th November 2007

We went to a wedding in Wales earlier this year and they had a barn dance, or 'Ceilidh' (pronounced 'kay-lee'). Generally speaking, this involved starting in one place, with your partner, before running off in opposite directions, skipping around for twenty minutes or so, then finally arriving back with your partner where you started. A Ceilidh. All good fun. The reason I mention this is that this is just what I did with Nicky in Waitrose yesterday. I like to call it the Waitrose Ceilidh. We start generally in the same position. Now, Nicky can handle the pointy elbows of the middle classes; I can't. If I come across people who've stopped, I do not ask them politely to move; I feel it necessary to do a complete u-turn, going in the opposite direction to the way I actually want to go, going down the next aisle, before meeting up with Nicky again, her clutching a tin of sweetcorn and me with a new Carlsberg Beer called Carlsberg Edge. If you've ever done any country dancing at school, I think you'll see the similarity. The Waitrose Ceilidh. Anyway, time to tackle the unadvertised England Manager job. I had to set up an FA Number (or 'FAN'), which I've done, now it's time to let them know what I'm capable of in an email to the Chief Executive –

Dear Brian Barwick

I noticed through the media over the past few

days that there is a vacancy for England Manager. I would like to apply for the position. Firstly, I have recently been considered for the Manager of Tottenham Hotspur, before they (wrongly in my opinion) gave it to Juande Ramos. I would also point out that I watched the match on Wednesday, and I listened to the pundits at half time. I did not go and make a cup of tea like everyone else, so I feel that I am a student of the game. Let me highlight an issue that I think is a problem with the English game. Everyone talks about the Christmas Tree Formation; 4-3-2-1. This is never going to work! How can you expect to not concede goals if you only have one person at the back? No, I propose a Reverse Christmas Tree Formation (RCTF). You have four people at the back, three people in front of them, followed by another two people, and then a lone striker. I think it is an idea right from the top drawer! I hope that you would consider my application; however, I would point out that I could only accept the position, if I could bring my colleague, Simon, with me as Assistant Coach. I have attached my CV for your perusal, and I look forward to hearing from you soon.

Kind regards

Ian Carpenter

Monday 26th November 2007

Dear Supporter

Thank you for contacting <u>FootballforAll@TheFA.com</u>

This email address is strictly reserved for those wishing to report allegations of abuse or discrimination such as incidents of racism or homophobia. Please note that we are unable to respond to any other type of query sent to this email address. If you have a football related query or comment you would like to make but do not wish to report an incident of discrimination please contact The FA Customer Relations Unit via the link below who will be happy to help:

<u>http://www.TheFA.com/Feedback</u>

Kind regards,

Customer Relations Unit
The Football Association

Naturally, I resent my original email. Soon afterwards, I got this reply:

Thank you for contacting The FA.

The FA's Customer Relations team will strive to respond within five working days of receipt. If further information is required, a comprehensive response will be sent within a further ten working days.

If you require a more urgent response you can contact the Customer Relations team on 020 7745 4545 between 9.15am and 5.00pm on weekdays.

To return to TheFA.com please click <u>here</u>

Kind regards,

The FA's Customer Relations team

OK, now we're getting somewhere. On with the jobs: Stonewall, the gay rights people, wanted a Senior Communications Officer and Major Donor and Corporate Accounts Manager – charity, sadly, and ABD: 17/10/07. SAM Learning – ABD: 12/10/07. University of Central Lancashire – ABD: 12/10/07. This is rubbish. I thought this page looked really exciting. Here's a nice blue advert:

Would you want to write for a traditionally tight-lipped, strait-laced firm of builders?

I might.

Let us know why, including details about your education, experience and skills.

OK I will –

Dear Carol

I noticed with interest your advertisement for a writer in the Guardian dated 29/09/07. I would like to be a writer, except I find that I get a bit stuck for things to say sometimes. That would probably not help. Anyway, you asked that I send details about my education, experience, and skills. I have attached my CV for your perusal. I would just like to say, that the choice of blue for your advert was inspired! All the other adverts on page 17 of the Guardian dated 29/09/07 were monochrome and boring. I look forward to hearing from you soon.

Kind regards

Ian Carpenter

PS I have also attached a picture of the recent bowls final, which I took from my dining room chair. It is also blue!

Tuesday 27th November 2007

Today I received my first Christmas card of the year from Sacha in the office. It's not even December! Well, I say Christmas card, but it was more of a Christmas Post-it note. Also got an email from the tight-lipped, straight-laced builders:

Dear Ian

Thank you for your application for the above position. Regretfully the vacancy has now been filled, but your interest is appreciated. Best of luck for the future.

Kind regards

Carol

Carol Parsons
PA to Chief Executive

That was nice. She wished me all the best of luck for the future. I think it must have been the picture of the bowls final that put her off. Admin' over, on with the jobs: Senior Press Officer for CIPD:

What does the future of work look like? How can firms win the war for talent? Are migrant workers the answer to the skills shortages firms face today? What role do

flexible working, diversity, employer branding, pay and pensions have to play in motivating people at work?

Interesting. I have heard of this new craze for branding. Some people, for some reason, have taken to getting themselves branded with hot irons. Fair enough if you want to do it to yourself, but to brand your boss...? Surely that's going a bit too far? Anyway, the closing date was 8/10/07. The Brooklands Group are looking for a Circulation and Marketing Manager:

Responsibilities will include planning and executing retail and added value promotions as well as subs renewal and acquisition programmes. He/she will be creative, literate and numerate.

I guess you might have to be literate if you're planning an acquisitions programme. They offer:

Generous basic salaries
Five weeks' holiday
Travelcard loan scheme
Bupa private medical insurance*
Stakeholder pension plan*
Free chocolate on Fridays!

* Medical insurance and pension benefits apply from six month anniversary of joining date.

Ah, but the free chocolate is from week one! –

Dear Sue

I note with renewed interest your advertisements in the Guardian dated 29/09/07. I would like to apply for all three positions advertised. They were:

Circulation and Marketing Manager

PR Manager (magazines, events, corporate)

Sponsorship Manager

Please find attached my CV for your perusal. I would be grateful if you could clarify one thing. Why do you have to wait six months for the medical and insurance benefits, whereas you get the free chocolate immediately? I only mention this, because I was in Waitrose over the weekend, and they had a bar of chocolate that was £6.50. £6.50 for a bar of chocolate?!? I look forward to hearing from you soon.

Kind regards

Ian Carpenter

There's been political scandal today, over alleged donations given to the Labour Party by David Abrahams through third parties. £700,000 apparently. It got me thinking about the old drinking song 'Father Abraham' –

David Abrahams
Had seven hundred thousand pounds
Seven hundred thousand pounds had David Abrahams

And he didn't laugh
And he didn't cry
All he did was go like this...

Maybe not. Anyway, Emma in the office highlighted another news story she thought might have been of some interest to me: The Scotland Manager, Alex McLeish has vacated his position for Birmingham City. Hmmm.

Wednesday 28th November 2007

No administration tonight – phew! I spent the day stuck in various traffic jams around the East End of London. They were doing some gas works outside Aldgate East Tube Station. All very well and good, but it took me two hours to get to Shoreditch. Why did I drive? After meeting with a representative from the water board, it was decided that rather than fix the low pressure in a block of flats that I manage, he would go off to speak to his area manager. Great. Thank you very much. The A13 back to Basildon was pretty poor too. And not a single Nobby or Stobby. Not a great day. Anyway, on with the jobs: Marcus Evans want International Sales Executives:

To succeed at marcus evans you will require:
Excellent written and verbal conversation skills.

In addition to the above marcus evans will provide:
International transfer opportunities to Asia, Australia, Africa, Europe, and America both for short term

Both five places? Where are *their* written skills? –

```
Dear Recruitment Manager

I quote 'ref SR09'. I am writing regarding your
positions advertised in The Guardian dated 29/09/07.
I realise that I am applying almost two months
```

late, it is a long story. Anyway, I would like to apply for your positions. I have a long history in sales, and I have also lived in mainland Europe for a couple of years. I have attached my CV for your perusal, and I look forward to hearing from you soon.

Kind regards

Ian Carpenter

And one for a Researcher/Assistant: 'Very Intelligent, quick, flexible, accurate, media-literate person wanted for part-time research'. No company name or location given.

Hmm –

Dear Caroline

I read with a not inconsiderable amount of interest your advert in the Guardian dated 29/09/07. I am fairly intelligent, I am quite slow though. I am flexible (apart from my back), I am quite accurate, and I am media-literate (I do read, listen, and watch several TV programmes). Am I the sort of person you would be interested in? I have attached my CV for your perusal, and I look forward to hearing from you soon.

Kind regards

Ian Carpenter

Pickering Chatto? – ABD: 8/10/07. And the Scottish FA have said on TV that they'd prefer a Scottish person for their job. I suppose I could try an accent...? No.

Friday 30th November 2007

I received a phone call at 9.30 this morning at work from my parents. My Uncle Glyn died last night in his sleep. He was only 59 years old. It shocked me, to be quite honest. It was completely unexpected. I am very upset. A line from Tom Stoppard's *Rosencrantz and Guildenstern are Dead* comes to mind:

> For all the compasses in the world, there's only
> one direction, and time is its only measure

Time is indeed its only measure, and it was too short for my Uncle Glyn. So I am going to raise a glass to him tonight. I didn't see him very often, but I miss him.

[Cuts have been made to the remainder of the text. See endnote. Ed.]

Saturday 1st December 2007

Mr Site wants a PR executive, contact jobs@mrsite.co.uk –

```
Dear Madam/Sir

I noted, with pre-seasonal Christmas joy, your
advert in the Guardian dated 29/09/07. How did
you possibly obtain the website mrsite.co.uk? Did
you not have competition from other people? I
don't know anyone called Mrs Ite, but I am sure
they would be interested in your domain name. I
have attached my CV for your perusal, and I look
forward to hearing from you soon.

Kind regards

Ian Carpenter
```

And the UK Film Council want a Diversity Executive:

With you excellent knowledge and understanding of diversity, access and inclusion issues, and a strong track record of delivering diversity strategies and programmes you will be expected to provide expert advice and support to the UKFC.

Ok, my advice: never order the great big bucket of chicken. ABD: 15/10/07. Audley Travel want Country Specialists – brilliant, I was born in the Forest of Dean, which is proper country:

If you are applying for a Country Specialist role, please include your travel history with dates and durations.

Hmmm –

Dear Madam/Sir

I read your advert in the Guardian dated 29/09/07. I was mesmerised by the image of the mill from which you work. I am a country specialist. I was born in the Forest of Dean, and that really is in the country. I used to play army with a friend of mine, called Paul Watkins in the ferns. It was all good fun. Anyway, I attach my CV for your perusal, and I look forward to hearing from you soon.

Kind regards

Ian Carpenter

Monday 3rd December 2007

We've instigated a new system at the office. For the past several months, whenever Simon and I are leaving the office for lunch or whatever, there's been an awkward moment at the door. It's a bit like the Chuckle Brothers – 'No you first, no after you, no really I insist' etc. What we have now instigated is a Four Week Rotational System. Let me explain this. There are five days in a week; given. Monday, Tuesday, and Wednesday do not have an 'r' in them, whereas Thursday and Friday do. So, on a Monday, Tuesday, and Wednesday, Simon goes through the door first. On a Thursday and Friday, I go through the door first, quite simple. However, more observant readers will have noticed that Simon gets to go through the door first on three days and me on only two. This is where the Four Week Rotational System comes into play (and I intend to use this in my forthcoming interview with Brian Barwick for the England Manager job). The way it works is for the first week, it is Simon with the Monday, Tuesday, Wednesday three-day bias. The second week it's me with the MTW three-day bias. I keep the three-day bias in the third week, before Simon gets it back in the fourth week, thus completing the cycle. Brilliant! And it worked for the whole day today. There was no awkwardness at the door or anything. Anyway, an email:

Dear Ian,

Thank you for sending me your CV and applying for International Sales Executive position (through Careers UK). I have been trying to reach you over the phone, but unfortunately I was not successful.

Ian, the position we are recruiting for is telephone based position in the office in Central London (telesales). We are contacting senior decision makers in Banking, Finance and Insurance Industry across Europe. It is a full time job (Mon-Fri). To begin with, please visit our websites www.marcusevans.com (this will give you an understanding of the company mission, profile, values, when we started, global offices and all of the different services we provide) and www.mefinance.com (to understand different Banking, Finance & Insurance conferences we offer our clients).

From this research we can have an initial phone based interview to tell you more about the company and also for me to understand your career prospects and requirements.

Please call me tomorrow to arrange your phone screen interview.

Regards,

Dagmar Grekcova
MARCUS EVANS conferences
Banking, Finance & Insurance Division Europe

How exciting! I applied for their job two months late, and they still want me to call them! I've been doing this for over two months and have had just one human contact, with Lesley-Ann from tenUK. I'm really excited – not that I want the job, you understand, but it's a real human contact! I can't wait to phone them tomorrow.

Tuesday 4th December 2007

From The Brooklands Group:

Dear Ian

Thank you for your email in response to our recruitment advertisement in the Guardian of 29th September. All three vacancies have now been successfully recruited, so we are unable to process your application. Thank you for your interest in Brooklands Group, we wish you every success for the future.

Regards,

Sue

No mention of the chocolate? I'm not having that –

Dear Sue

Thank you for your email. I am sorry that all three positions have now been recruited. I would still like to know why you get free chocolates immediately, but have to wait for the medical and insurance benefits. I look forward to hearing from you soon.

Kind regards

Ian Carpenter

Friday 7th December 2007

I still haven't phoned Dagmar, so at this point I think I'd better send an email –

Dear Dagmar

Thank you for your email, which has given me great encouragement. I have watched your staff video on your website. It seems to me that the main motivation of your staff is money. Have you heard of Maslow's theory of motivation? He argues that we have nine needs:

1. Biological: i.e food, air, etc.

2. Safety needs

3. Affiliation needs (having a mate to go down the pub with)

4. Esteem (feeling like you are doing alright thank you)

5. The need to know and understand

6. Aesthetic needs

7. Transcendence

8. Freedom of enquiry or expression

9. Self Actualization

It seems that most of the people on your staff video are not interested in self-actualization, only money. Could you please clarify whether marcusevans would consider other needs outside wealth? I am very interested in your linguarama programme, and look forward to hearing from you soon.

Kind regards

Ian Carpenter

Saturday 8th December 2007

What's this? A second ad from Marcus Evans?:

Ideal candidates will have experience from an agency background, and SPSS/quanvert experience would be beneficial amongst quant researchers.

Maybe I should get in touch with Dagmar? No, the ad says to contact Martin, OK –

```
Dear Martin

I read with some bewilderment your advert in the
Guardian dated 29/09/07. I say bewilderment, because
I have recently applied for another job in your
organisation. The person dealing with my other
application is Dagmar Greckova. Do you both work
in the same office? I would like to apply for your
positions. Admittedly, I do not know what you mean
when you say quanvert experience, but I am willing
to learn. Please find attached my CV for your perusal.
If you have any further queries, please either speak
to Ms Greckova, or contact me directly.

Kind regards

Ian Carpenter
```

Sunday 9th December 2007

We are just about to set off to Gloucester, as Uncle Glyn's funeral is tomorrow. I am really not looking forward to it. It's a four-hour drive, and then I'll have to deal with that whole family grief thing. The whole thing is simply rubbish. I'll take my Guardian Work with me as a comfort blanket. My mum and dad will probably think I'm barmy, but hey ho, what are you gonna do? Furthermore, just think of the Nobby versus Stobby potential on a 360-mile round trip.

Tuesday 11th December 2007

I think I've touched a nerve with the people at Marcus Evans:

Dear Ian,

To clarify the motivation of the people working in ME: money, career progression, challenge and friendly, but busy working environment. I believe you have seen our values on our website - quality, energy, proactive and success - that is what we believe in and require from our employees.

As in the all the sales jobs, we are looking for hungry people as well, someone who does not want to take home basic salary, but is getting great commission on the top. As you are successful, company is growing and successful as well. Our company is trying to motivate you by 1.money you could earn, 2. career (and possibility of international transfer or in between our departments).

At the moment I am looking for another member for my team – conference sales in Banking, Finance and Insurance Division, to contact senior decision makers in this area. Please let me know if you would be interested in this position or I should pass your CV for our Linguarama training department (as you mentioned in your email).

Best regards,

Dagmar Grekcova

Clear as a bell —

Dear Dagmar

Thank you for your email. I note from your tone, that I may have upset you with my comments about people only wanting money at ME. Please accept my apologies, as this was not my intention. I would still like to be considered for your position in the conference sales division. Although I am interested in the Linguarama position, I would rather see this application through for the moment. I was trying to think of some way that we could work with the values - quality, energy, proactive, and success. How about QUEPS!? Or even PEQS!? I think it needs some work. Please let me know your earliest thoughts, and I look forward to hearing from you soon.

Kind regards

Ian Carpenter

Wednesday 12th December 2007

Dear Ian,

Thank you for your email and your feedback. We have found other candidates more suitable to the role that we are recruiting for, so at this moment I would like to say that you have been unsuccessful.

I wish you all the best with your career prospective.

Best regards,

Dagmar

'Career prospective'? Next email:

** *THIS IS AN AUTOMATED MESSAGE – REPLIES WILL NOT BE RECEIVED* **

Dear Ian

Thank you for your recent application for Leaders for Business 2008 which we have now been able to review in greater detail.

Due to very strong competition for this vacancy, we regret to advise you that after careful consideration, our decision is not to take your application further on this occasion.

Should you wish to re-apply for a similar position again in the future, please note we cannot accept another application within one year.

Due to the high volume of applications we are unable to offer feedback.

May we thank you for the time you have given us and wish you every success in the future.

Yours sincerely

British Airways Recruitment

I have to be honest, I can't really remember applying to BA. This has, however, raised an important point. I will probably be put on the 'never give a job interview to this person' list of all the companies that advertised in The Guardian dated 29/09/07. This might be a problem at some point...

Thursday 13th December 2007

I got back from work today at around 7.30pm to be greeted, on opening the door, by Hippy. Now this may seem like a picture of domestic bliss, but it really wasn't. It meant that Hippy had been locked in the house since 7 o'clock this morning. Which meant that I was likely to find some feline doings somewhere in the house – normally, for some unknown reason, in the bath. However, the milk of feline kindness shone on me this evening, as she had not done anything anywhere. She really is such a good cat.

Remember Phyllis, of 'Mum and Phyllis' fame? The toaster? Here's a picture of Phyllis holding my copy of the Guardian work pages dated 29/09/07:

That paper's been all over Europe. It's been to a Swiss Bank in Geneva; up a very tall mountain in France; to my Mum and Dad's kitchen in the Royal Forest of Dean — what a journey for a thing that normally gets promptly slung in the recycling bin. OK, down to work —

Dear Brian Barwick

As you will recall, I applied for the position of England Manager on the 25th November 2007. I subsequently received a message from you indicating that I had sent my email to the wrong department, and so I resent my application on the 26th November 2007. You will also recall that I have recently been considered for the vacancy at Tottenham Hotspur before (wrongly in my opinion) they gave it to Juande Ramos. Can you imagine my dismay, when on the way to work this morning, I hear that you are giving the job to Fabio Capello? I have not even had an acknowledgement to my application of the 25th and 26th November 2007. How can you possibly be considering filling a job role, when you have not even spoken to all of the applicants? Now, I have to admit that, I do not have as much football experience of Mr Capello. However, I did offer you the incentive of bringing my colleague, Simon, as Assistant Coach. Since then, I have acquired the commitment of a work

associate, Barry, who will be prepared to take
on the ground-keeping of Wembley Stadium. Anyway,
please do not make any hasty decisions tomorrow
morning. I look forward to hearing from you first
thing in the morning.

Kind regards

Ian Carpenter

Honestly, who do they think they are at the FA, I ask you?

Monday 17th December 2007

Today I received my first real letter, on actual paper, since beginning my project! It's from Audley travel:

Dear Ian

Thank you for your interest in Working for Audley Travel and for taking the time to forward your details to us.

We have read through your CV in detail and whilst some of your skills and experience are relevant, they do not quite match those we currently require for the business at this time. Therefore, we will not be processing your application further.

Ian, I would like to take this opportunity to thank you again for your interest in Audley Travel and I wish you every success in your future career.

Yours sincerely

Human Resources Co-ordinator
Audley Travel Ltd

Oh well. I reckon I might have made their shortlist, though.

Wednesday 19th December 2007

We put up our Christmas tree tonight. Yes, I know it is a little late, but we have been a bit busy recently. We went to the shops after work, as we did not have any Christmas tree lights. I don't think the people in the shops could believe we were still looking for Christmas tree lights. Well, in our house we believe in the six days of Christmas; after all it only takes half as long. Then, we can sit on the bus with Lenny, and buy bread, petrol etc., without being beaten around the ribcage with the aforementioned pointy elbows of the middle classes. Anyway, we were after the plain white tree lights that you can get. However, the only ones left were snooker balls on a string.

Nature Publishing Group:

No experience?
First Office Job?

You should be a new Graduate with good A Level and GCSE grades to join our busy recruitment office. The work is varied and will include general administrative duties, liaising with candidates and clients as well as answering telephone and email enquiries and you must be able to work on your own initiative.

You don't need to be a graduate in order to punctuate

properly. Well past the apply by date, but –

Dear Katy

I read your advert in the Guardian dated 29/09/07.
I have to admit that your sentences were a bit
long and I think that they may have needed some
punctuation but I am willing to overlook this as
I would like to apply for your position anyway
and have attached my curriculum vitae for your
perusal if you would not mind reading it at all.
I look forward to hearing from you soon.

Kind regards

Ian Carpenter

Thursday 20th December 2007

Dear Ian

Thank you for your application, but unfortunately
the position has been filled.

Best of luck with your search.

Regards

Katy Edwards
Recruitment Administrator
Beechwood Recruitment Limited

I don't believe them, but never mind. The Lounge Group
are recruiting 'Full time students seeking P/T promotional
work (Non-students can also apply)'. They are a trendy
marketing agency that are targeting the under 35 market.
They promote things at Universities and clubs, and their
website is full of pictures of bright young things having a
marvellous time. OK –

Dear all at the lounge group.

Your advert in the Guardian dated 29/09/07 left
me with a feeling like I had just eaten a sherbet
lemon. I am not a student anymore, but your advert
said that I can apply anyway. I have to tell you
that I am 35 years old next August, so I will be

outside of your target age range, does this make a difference? I notice from your website that a lot of your promotions take place in nightclubs. I haven't been to a nightclub in years. We prefer to have people around for a few nibbles and drinks. I find that you can't have a decent conversation in a nightclub, as the music is just too loud. However, I attach my CV for your perusal and I look forward to hearing from you soon.

Kind regards

Ian Carpenter

I sent that one 4.20 and got this back at 6:

Dear Ian,

The Lounge Group is a Marketing and PR agency which specialises in the under 35s demographic. While our campaigns aim to target this demographic this does not exclude those over 35s from joining our network of field staff. Although the advert was aimed to target students as we were hoping to recruit candidates for specific campaigns (i.e. those on university campuses) we review every application on its own merits and consider applicants from all walks of life. It is true that some of our campaigns are held at night clubs

but the vast majority are not. We have closed
our applications for this year but will consider
your application early in the New Year.

Kind regards and Season's Greetings

Nic Fine
Operations Executive

Very decent of you, Nic.

Monday 24th December 2007

I have discovered the origins of the Mornington Crescent game. My Mother in Law bought me a book on Mah Jongg. The connection is obvious. Take these rules for example: when a player completes a hand by robbing a kong of two bamboos, they score a full hand, which is known as 'Scratching a Carrying Pole'. And if a player completes a kong and with the tile obtained they complete another kong and then, with the second tile, they obtain 'Mah Jongg'; then – so long as the two kongs and the whole hand are completed in a single turn – they again score a full hand and this is called 'Kong upon Kong' or 'Twofold Fortune'. That's put me in the mood –

Winchmore Hill.

Thursday 3rd January 2008

TNT Magazine wants a Deputy Sales Manager and an Events Marketing Executive: 'You will need previous media sales experience, excellent account management skills and the ability to lead a team.' OK –

Dear Madam/Sir

I read with alacrity your advert for the above roles in the Guardian dated 29/09/07. I appreciate that I am slightly tardy in my application, but would like to apply for the two positions advertised. You stipulated that I may need previous media sales experience. Well, on December 30th, the film Babe was on the telly. My partner did not want to watch it at first, but I managed to sell it to her. In the end she quite enjoyed it! Moreover, she is a vegetarian! I also have excellent account management skills. I once managed to avoid being charged for an excess overdraft fee, by using the internet. I have experience in leading a team. On December 30th (sorry to repeat myself), there was a film on after Babe called Snow Dogs. He had to lead a team of husky dogs in order to pull his sled. The funny thing was, he kept tripping over the lead! Anyway, I have attached my CV for your

perusal, and I look forward to hearing from you
soon.

Kind regards

Ian Carpenter

Friday 4th January 2008

Chelsea Square are looking for a Designer/Specifier:

Working mainly on refurbishments of Victorian Properties, the successful candidate will be conversant with autoCAD, possess a high level of design creativity encompassing spatial awareness

'autoCAD'? I'll give it a go –

Dear Michael

I fumbled across your advert in the Guardian dated 29/09/07. I would like to apply for your position as Designer/Specifier. I can not confess to be conversant with autoCAD. Is this one of those new computer games that you can talk to? I do not know of it, but I am willing to learn. I do have a high level of design creativity, and a great deal of spatial awareness. In my opinion, Ursa Major looks nothing like a great bear, and as for the hunter Orion, I ask you. I have attached my CV for your perusal, and I look forward to hearing from you soon.

Kind regards

Ian Carpenter

Contemporary Design Gallery London... Hang on, this sounds like another scam –

Dear Madam/Sir

I read with some concern your advert in the Guardian dated 29/09/07. I say this because I applied for a similar position, from a similar sized advert, in the same paper. It was on page 9 towards the bottom of the paper. It turned out to be a scam! Can you assure me that, before I send my CV, this is a genuine job opportunity?

Kind regards

Ian Carpenter

Better to be safe than sorry.

Saturday 5th January 2008

Absolute Appointments were looking for Media Sales
people –

Dear Simon or Claire

I am writing following your recent advert in the
Guardian dated 29/09/07. You said that I could
spice up 2007 with a career in media sales.
However, it is now 2008; can this year be spiced
up in the same manner? I look forward to hearing
from you soon.

Kind regards

Ian Carpenter

Monday 7th January 2007

From Claire, the Director of Absolute Appointments, sent on Sunday Morning:

Morning Ian

Please can you send your CV to us and we will give you a call

From Simon, the other Director of Absolute Appointments on Monday Morning:

Please forward your CV by return and we will call you for an initial telephone interview.

Oh. Schoolboy error – they're a recruitment company... But they both got back to me... maybe I better have a look... Foxtons! I've been trying to avoid being employed by Foxtons, but now they're trying another angle. Cunning. They're looking for an image retoucher. Sounds a bit wrong to me, but –

Dear Harriet

I noted your advert in the Guardian dated 29/09/07. I appreciate that I am a bit late in applying, but I would like to apply anyway. This is in spite of the fact that I have no Photoshop skills, no knowledge of Quark Express, Illustrator or

Acrobat. I have attached my CV for your perusal
and I look forward to hearing from you soon.

Kind regards

Ian Carpenter

Thursday 17th January 2008

Some fantastic news for spider lovers: the smoking spider must have reproduced before she popped her spider clogs from spider lung cancer! There's a new diddy spider that comes to the back window – that charming suitor spider must have moved fast and got in there just in time.

No responses from job applications today... apart from a message on my answer machine from Harriet at Foxtons. Now forgive me, dear reader, but are these people mad? They want me to call them to discuss my application. This could be interesting –

Me: Hello, I am returning your message.

Harriet: Yes, you want to be an image retoucher?

Me: Well, not really.

Harriet: Your application mentioned you do not have any of the skills that we require.

Me: Nope, I do not have the skills that you require.

Harriet: Great! When can you start?

I'll try to call her from the office tomorrow.

Saturday 19th January 2008

This morning I received a fantastic reply from Chelsea Square:

Ian,

Thank you for stumbling across our advert. I'm sorry for the late reply but have only just been discharged after my gender change operation. I am afraid we have filled the position, but we would like to offer you opportunity to apply for the vacancy of hole punch assistant. This is a part time position offering 36 minutes a week and feel that with your strong creativity skills you would be the ideal candidate. The salary is pro rata 50p per annum and you will of course be required to work shifts which shall include nights.

Please feel free to drop me a line should you have any questions.

Kind Regards

Michael Lansley

Congratulations Michael, you have just joined Tottenham Hotspur and Patrick Meiier in a very exclusive club indeed.

Tuesday 22nd January 2008

The University of Manchester wanted a 'MIMAS development officer (Geodata Services Software engineer)'. Thanks for the clarification –

Dear Madam/Sir

I came across your advert in the Guardian dated 29/09/07. I appreciate that the apply-by date has long passed, but I had a few questions regarding your advert. Firstly, I would like to congratulate your University Challenge team for beating Trinity College Cambridge yesterday on BBC2. Secondly, I would be grateful if you could clarify what MIMAS stands for. I look forward to your earliest response.

Kind regards

Ian Carpenter

Wednesday 23rd January 2008

Dear Ian

MIMAS stands for Manchester Information & Associated Services and is based at University of Manchester.

For further info please see their website here: http://www.mimas.ac.ukhttp://www.mimas.ac.uk

Best regards

Adam West
Central HR Admin Assistant

Help the planet to chill out - don't print this unless strictly necessary

Adam West? Surely not *the* Adam West, the original Caped Crusader? Seems unlikely. Hmmm, still not clear –

Dear Adam

Thank you for your reply. I'm still a bit unsure as to why it is MIMAS and not just MIAS. Where do you get the extra M from? If you take the & symbol as an A, it should be MIAAS. I look forward to hearing from you soon.

Kind regards

Ian Carpenter

PS My Dad went to Manchester University

And this little gem from my boss –

Southend to Brentford and back

22 Jan 08

Dear Ian

On the A127 it occured to me that the Norbert Dentressangle v Eddie Stobart game is dangerous. Particularly as it encourages driving without due care and attention. I decided not to play.

I then discovered it is now physically impossible not to play. Try it. It's like eating a sugar donut without licking your lips. Impossible.

Things looked promising with Stobby maintaining the lead until I reach Nobbyland betwix A10 and A12 on the return when the score went from an amazing 10-10 to a soul destroying 15-10 to Nobby. Luckily I didn't get arrested or killed.

Steve

Friday 25th January 2008

Dear Ian

The letters stand for Manchester Information & Associated Services. The word 'and' is very rarely included in acronyms such as this, and in this case I think they would simply have wanted to make the acronym easy to pronounce.

Best regards

Adam West
Central HR Admin Assistant

Help the planet to chill out - don't print this unless strictly necessary

Hmmm. Definitely not *that* Adam West. OK –

Dear Adam

Thank you for your email. I agree the word 'and' is very rarely included in an acronym. Also, not generally included in an acronym is a letter in the middle of a word. If we allow letters in the middle of words to form part of the acronym, then 'Liverpool Football Club' or 'LFC' could become 'LFOC'. LFOC is much easier to pronounce than LFC. I look forward to your thoughts on this matter.

Kind regards

Ian Carpenter

Saturday 26th January 2008

I have decided to bring a fresh viewpoint to the ongoing acronym debate between me and Manchester University –

```
Liverpool Football Club
Anfield
Liverpool
```

Dear Madam/Sir

I am a keen supporter of Liverpool Football Club. I have attached a copy of recent correspondence with Manchester University regarding acronyms. I would be grateful if you could provide us with your opinion on the LFC versus LFOC debate. Could LFOC work for you? I mean, it would involve changing all of your merchandise, and replacing most of the seats in The KOP, but as a concept? I look forward to hearing your thoughts on this matter.

Kind regards

Ian Carpenter

Wednesday 6th February 2008

JML, the shopping channel, has positions. I did a bit of research for this one –

Dear Maria

I felt like I was jumping off the high diving board when I saw your advert in the Guardian dated 29/09/07. I appreciate that I am late in applying, but I would like to apply for your positions. I have carried out extensive research on your three channels. Tonight, for example, you were selling the Nicer Dicer on Channel 631, the Easy Stitch on 632 and on Channel 657 you were selling the Dri-Buddi. I would like to submit a new product for your shopping channel: the No-Inky-Pinky!

You know when you read a newspaper, your fingers get covered in ink? Well here is the solution: a patented (well not quite yet) set of rubber gloves that protect your hands from ink stains when reading a paper. It is at a very early stage in development, and I would welcome your suggestions for improvement. I reckon the retail value would be around £11.97 (but you could do two for £23.75). I have attached my CV for your perusal, and I look forward to hearing from you soon.

Kind Regards

Ian Carpenter

There are only six jobs left – I'm on the final straight!

Thursday 7th February 2008

When I was at school, I played Rozencrantz in *Rosencrantz and Guildenstern are Dead*. In the opening scene I had to toss a coin and have it land heads up time after time. We tried a double headed coin, a piece of wood; all sorts. In the end we decided it was better to mime the coin tossing. I mention this because of something that happened at work today: I'd previously spoken with Simon about the Derren Brown Programme 'The System', during which he tossed a coin heads ten times in a row. Apparently it took him over nine hours of solid coin tossing. While clearing my desk of paperwork, I came across a two pence piece and thought I'd give it a go myself –

First throw:
Heads.

Second throw:
Heads.

Third throw:
Heads.

Blimey I'm really on to something here. I needn't have mimed all those years ago.

Fourth throw:

Tails.

Pants. I tossed the coin to Simon to see if he could do any better. He was in the middle of a telephone call, so it had to wait.

First throw:
Heads.

Second throw:
Heads.

Third throw:
Heads.

Fouth throw:
Heads.

Fifth throw:
Heads.

I am starting to take interest now.

Sixth, seventh, and eighth throw:
All heads.

All these throws have been interrupted by telephone calls etc.

Ninth throw:
Heads.

I'm trying not to believe that this is happening.

Tenth and final throw:
Heads!

It took Derren Brown nine hours of filming, and Simon did it on his first attempt. Amazing! Anyway, Sophie Macpherson Ltd. are looking for experienced registrars –

Dear Madam/Sir

I noticed your advert in the Guardian dated 29/09/07, with a feeling that I had just skipped a stone seven times on the sea. You mentioned that only experienced registrars need apply. Sorry, I am not an experienced registrar, but I would like to apply anyway. Please find attached my CV. I look forwards to hearing from you soon.

Kind regards

Ian Carpenter

Later, this came back:

Dear Ian,

Thank you very much for sending in your CV to Sophie Macpherson Ltd. I have passed it to my colleagues (noting your particular interest!) for review and should a position suitable to your interests and experience arise, they will be in contact with you. If you do not object we will also keep your details on file for future reference. If you have any further queries then please do not hesitate to contact us. We wish you every success in your search and hope we can be of assistance.

Kind regards

Fantastic! No other responses, so on with the jobs: Aldi keep writing to me. Every week I receive an email for their Area Manager positions. They now have an advert on the final page of my quest for, well, Area Managers –

Dear Madam/Sir

I saw your advert in the Guardian dated 29/09/07. I have applied for every other advert in the newspaper, but I have not had one interview, as yet. I hope that your job will be different. I look forward to your earliest response.

Kind regards

Ian Carpenter

Plantech were looking for an IT Trainee – APD 9/10/2007. Media Contacts – recruitment consultants. The Chesterfield and North East Derbyshire Council for Voluntary Service & Action Ltd. (their Acronym would be CNEDCVCSA. It rolls of the tongue, doesn't it?) – charity, I'm afraid. Norfolk Dance were looking for a Director – APD 29/10/07. OK. Final job! Nearly six month's work and here it comes. This is it; this is the end of the quest. I can't do it now, can I? No, because Question Time is on. I'll do it tomorrow.

Friday 9th February 2008

There are a finite number of jobs in the Guardian work pages dated 29/09/07. It had to end at some time. It could have ended last night. I chose not to end it. So it was with a heavy heart that I woke up this morning and realised that this may be it. This may be the final day of Guardianwork. I went downstairs, and we'd run out of Douwe Egberts coffee. Pants. I had to drink the Nescafé that's there for emergencies. I went up to have a shower, and guess what? No shower gel. It was then that I recognised Nicky's genius for supermarket shopping: tiare flower and patchouli hand wash is a lot more useful when you need a wash than a packet of cheese and onion crisps. So, here I am, ready to do the last job – oh, an email from Aldi:

Thank you for submitting your application to join the Area Manager Training Scheme. We will endeavour to respond within 14 days of receiving your application. In the meantime, may we take this opportunity to thank you for your interest in Aldi.

OK. This is it: The Yale University Press wants 'A Senior Publicist with one years trade experience handling your own books' and a 'Production Editor for illustrated list including Pevsner Architectural Guides'. OK –

Dear Katie

Did you realise that your advert was the last advert in the Guardian dated 29/09/07? Did you have to pay extra for that privilege? I note that you are looking for a Senior Publicist. You have asked for one year's experience of handling your own books. I do handle my own books, and have done on a regular basis. I like to categorise them into sections. For instance, I have a travel section, a poetry section, and a section for all of my annuals that I collect every year. My personal favourite is the Beano. I don't think that the Dandy quite cuts the mustard. You are also looking for a Production Editor. I would be grateful if you could provide more information on the Pevsner Architectural Guide, as I am not familiar with their work. I have enclosed my CV for your perusal, and I look forward to hearing from you soon.

Kind regards

Ian Carpenter

That's it!!!

THE END

It's all over.

I've done it.

I have applied for every job in the Guardian work pages dated 29/09/07. Well, apart from charity jobs, and some that had passed their apply by dates. I'm going to celebrate tonight. I may even open a bottle of Champagne, who knows? Let's see what happens...

Saturday 9th February 2008

I woke up this morning with a huge sense of achievement. I felt like a dolphin that has managed to swim through a dolphin-friendly tuna net. So what do I do now? I sent a text message to Simon and others, to let them know I've finished my Guardianwork project. I found my Guardian work pages dated 29/09/07 on the office desk and began wondering what I should do with it. Various people have offered suggestions along the way. I could frame it, but that seems a bit pointless really. I could recycle it. Emma once suggested that I make a giant origami sculpture out of it – now that would be interesting. I could make a crane the size of a, well, a crane. I don't know what to do. I'll ponder it while I am watching the Six Nations this afternoon. Barrynormal sent me a text:

Do I have to keep checking the blog for new entries or is that really it?

Well, I am afraid that that *is* it. There may be a few loose ends – I still have outstanding applications with a few people – but essentially I'm done.

Monday 11th February

Guess what? There's a bonus page. What I thought were just adverts on page thirty are, in fact, just that: they are adverts, adverts for jobs! Underneath the article about a software engineer from Harrogate called Paul Smith are some more job adverts (incidentally, Paul found the IT market tougher than he expected). It is a good thing that I didn't throw the paper in the recycling! OK: there are 'Luton Based Opportunities' with Vauxhall Motors. Sadly, it's through an agency. Graduate Recruitment – another agency. Got Jobs for Graduates – ditto. These adverts are not so good at all. PFJ – another agency. Brand and Brown are looking for a graduate to join their training programme:

Send us your CV, together with a 200-word newspaper style article (either fictitious or real) about an aspect of your university life.

That's more like it –

Dear Madam/Sir

I came across your advert in the Guardian dated 29/09/07, with a feeling like I had just eaten some Sharon fruit for the first time. You asked that I submit my CV with a 200 word article about my university life. Here is a description of my first encounter with my friend Garrett:

Garrett and I met for the first time at Bath University. I pitched up, with my Mum and Dad in tow on my first day. We all faffed around for a while, before my parents and entourage left me on my own, for the first time. It was very daunting. Stuck in a breeze-block room, that was so small, it was a lucky thing that I didn't have a cat that liked to be swung. Bambi-like, I timidly ventured out into the corridor. The first place I headed to was the communal toilets. As you do. Garrett was in the toilets/washroom, shaving. This area was shared between 26 student flats. You can imagine the state that this area found itself in after a few weeks. So Garrett was the first person I met in my new adult life.

Garrett: "Alright? My name is Garrett." (Extending his hand)

Me: "Yes I'm ok, my name is Ian." (Shaking Garrett's hand, yes I am a proper adult now)

Garrett: "Do you want a beer?"

Me: "Well ok then."

It was a bit more convoluted than that, but essentially Garrett and I were destined to be friends for a long time; that was 17 years ago.

I hope that you enjoy it.

Kind regards

Ian Carpenter

Now, the final – *final* – job is for Head of Global Risk Department with Merchant International:

A small but well-established corporate security and strategic risk consultancy is looking to hire a new head of the global risk department. The position requires a strong background in the political and strategic risk consulting arena with a focus on emerging markets. The successful candidate will manage a small team of researchers and have primary responsibility for developing new business and restructuring our product portfolio.

Here goes –

Dear Madam/Sir

I read with interest your advert for Head of Global Risk. I felt a bit like I had just taken a deep breath before a job interview. I am exceptionally good at Global Risk. Two Austrian friends of ours, Gert and Tina, once invited us over for a game.

I lost, but my strategy was very good. I think I was put off by the wiener schnitzel. Anyway, I have attached my CV for your perusal, and I look forward to hearing from you soon.

Kind regards

Ian Carpenter

That's it.

Done.

What do I do now?

Wednesday February 13th 2008

Yesterday I printed the entire project and presented it to Simon. When I printed it off, I picked up a pile of plain paper to put in the printer – just a random amount – and clicked print, and guess what? I'd put in the *exact* number of pages required to print it. Ten heads in a row is nothing compared to my paper picking abilities.

Blog to Book
A Note on the Text

In converting *Guardianwork* from blog to book, changes were made in order for it to work in the new medium. Generally speaking, this meant minor adjustments to avoid repetition and improve readability but towards the end considerable cuts were made in order to maintain the focus of the book. The original text is still online, in all its unexpurgated glory, waiting to welcome new converts and be scrutinised and deconstructed by academics. Since finishing the project, Ian Carpenter has added videos to his blog and updated it with further postings. I would urge any interested readers to have a look:

guardianwork.blogspot.com

Throughout the editing process, I worked closely with Carpenter, who assisted with the changes and proposed additional lines etc. As you might imagine, we had a lot of laughs.

Anthony Nott
Editor

Acknowledgements

I would like to express my thanks to the following people: Simon Bellamy, for agreeing to be my referee for the applications; Emyr Williams, for his support throughout this whole process; The Magnificent Six: Alison, Steve, Barry, and the other three – you know who you are; my parents, for all their help; Liz and Lez for a great holiday; the Swiss granny who knitted a pair of socks for Jean for Christmas; Jean for the Mah Jongg book; Anthony Nott, for a great editing job; and Nicky, who has been a rock throughout.

Ian Carpenter

Index

The
Beautiful
Group